NEW PENGUIN SHAKESPEARE

GENERAL EDITOR: T. J. B. SPENCER

NS3

WILLIAM

# CORIOLANUS

EDITED BY
G. R. HIBBARD

PENGUIN BOOKS

Birmingham Metropolitan College

139038

..., Harmondsworth, Middlesex, England
Penguin Bo... ...110 Ambassador Court, Baltimore, Maryland 21207, U.S.A.
Penguin Books Australia Ltd, Ringwood, Victoria, Australia

—

This edition first published in Penguin Books 1967
Reprinted 1968

—

This edition copyright © Penguin Books, 1967
Introduction and notes copyright © G. R. Hibbard, 1967

—

Made and printed in Great Britain by
Western Printing Services Ltd, Bristol
Set in Monotype Ehrhardt

This book is sold subject to the condition
that it shall not, by way of trade or otherwise,
be lent, re-sold, hired out, or otherwise circulated
without the publisher's prior consent in any form
of binding or cover other than that in which it is
published and without a similar condition
including this condition being imposed
on the subsequent purchaser

# CONTENTS

# INTRODUCTION

## 1

CORIOLANUS is a play of action, not reflection; its subject is strife and dissension. Five strands of irreconcilable conflict are tightly woven together to form the fabric of the plot. They are: first, the wars between the infant Roman republic and the neighbouring state of the Volsces; secondly, the intense personal rivalry between the hero, Rome's greatest soldier, and the Volscian leader, Tullus Aufidius; thirdly, the struggle for power within Rome itself between the patrician class, whose most intransigent member is Coriolanus, and the plebeians, organized and manipulated by their two Tribunes – Brutus and Sicinius; fourthly, the battle of wills between Coriolanus and his mother, Volumnia, over matters of political expediency; and, finally, the conflict within the hero himself when he is torn between a desire for revenge on the city that has rewarded his services to it with banishment, and the pull of the natural affection which he feels for his mother, his wife, and his young son.

The verse matches the action. Austere, rugged and often harsh, it is a perfect vehicle for the tirades, the exhortations, the eulogies and the accusations with which the play is filled. Almost devoid of lyricism, the poetry of *Coriolanus* has a hard, stony or metallic timbre that is peculiarly its own, as T. S. Eliot recognized when he began his poem 'Coriolan' with the words:

> *Stone, bronze, stone, steel, stone, oakleaves, horses' heels*
> *Over the paving.*

It is the poetry of public affairs, rather than of the heart and the inner world of private experience, making an insistent use of stark, antithetical statements in order to convey the absolute opposition of the 'contrarieties', as Shakespeare calls them, that he is dealing with, and the inability of most of the characters to see the issues they are faced with in any other terms than black and white. The characteristic note of the play is to be heard in such a line as that in which Aufidius sums up (IV.7.54) the instability of power:

> One fire drives out one fire; one nail one nail.

In *Coriolanus* the tone of a speech is quite as important as the imagery it employs. Many of the protagonist's diatribes are hurled at their audience in abrupt, stinging phrases that fall like a shower of stones from a catapult.

Yet this play, so strident with noises off stage as well as on, with the clash of arms on armour, with the shouts of the Roman mob and the impetuous harangues of the hero, is the most unified and symmetrical of all Shakespeare's tragedies. The source of its unity is the intense concentration on the figure of Coriolanus himself. When he is on the stage, as he is for the greater part of the play, he is the centre of interest and the focus of action; when he is not, he is invariably the subject of discussion, the target of plots, or the object of fears. His characteristic stance, whether one sees him in the theatre or in the mind's eye, is that of the solitary figure, the isolated individual, facing a hostile group of other men, driving them back with his sword, cowing them into submission with his scorn or inciting them to fury with his defiance. It is thus that he enters the play, and it is thus that he leaves it. Moreover, violent though the action is, his is the only death it leads to. The destructive, aggressive energy which he embodies in himself and stimulates in others discharges itself in the last scene with a complete finality. Some of Shakespeare's other tragedies raise even profounder issues than does this; some of his other tragic heroes – Hamlet, for example – engage the sympathies of an audience or a reader at a deeper level than Coriolanus can or is meant to, since he is presented in a way that inhibits the normal spectator from identifying himself with him; but in no other tragedy is the dramatist's mastery over the material at his disposal more assured and evident. *Coriolanus* is a long play, yet there is nothing loose or sprawling about it. All that happens and all that is said is strictly relevant to the total experience that it conveys.

And, because it has these qualities of shapeliness and completeness, because the passions it raises are released and spent in the last scene, this portrayal of strife and violence, of self-assertion confronting mob fury, and of instability in both the private and the public spheres, leaves a final impression of stillness and grandeur. It is like a great bronze statue, embodying in itself the values and the tensions of that Roman world which it represents. The achievements of the Roman republic were a consequence of its people's genius for warfare and for political organization. Behind their success in war lay their cult of *virtus* or valiancy, which, as Plutarch says in his *Life of Coriolanus*, 'was honoured in Rome above all other virtues'. At the root of their political cohesion was the value which they set on *pietas*, a sense of duty towards the family, the state, and the gods. Their civil life was conducted through public meetings and dominated by the practice of oratory. All these things find their place in the play. The hero himself cultivates *virtus* at the expense of everything else; his mother, at the climax of the tragedy, is *pietas* personified; and the most decisive actions in it are produced by the calculated exercise of rhetoric. Of the three Roman plays it is the most Roman, its author's tribute to, as well as his criticism of, a civilization which meant more to him and to his age than, perhaps, did any other.

Roman though it is, however, *Coriolanus* is also, like all good history, timeless. Shakespeare's success in bringing the Ancient World to life, in a way that his more learned contemporary Ben Jonson failed to do in his two Roman tragedies, is a direct result of his imaginative ability to connect it with his own times, and to interpret it in terms of activities and issues that were familiar to him and to his audience. Coriolanus is quite as much a Jacobean noble as he is a patrician of antique Rome. When the Second Officer, at the opening of II.2, speaks of the hero's 'noble carelessness', he is attributing to him the much prized quality of *sprezzatura*, that nonchalant ease of manner and studied contempt of popular opinion which was so carefully cultivated by the Elizabethan courtier. Shakespeare's England could provide many a public figure who had a great deal in common with the tempestuous and outspoken Roman soldier. Sir Walter Raleigh, to take only one example, had gone off to the French wars at the age of fourteen or so. His rapid rise to power and influence made him many enemies. Ballads accusing him of extortion and contempt for the poor were circulating in London about 1601, and when Aubrey described him as 'damnably proud' he was merely repeating a common complaint. A certain 'A.B.', writing to Lord Treasurer Burghley in 1586, at a time when Raleigh had been given control of the Cornish tin-mines and miners, finds fault with him for his lack of affability and expresses concern about its possible consequences in the event of a Spanish invasion. He says (Norman Lloyd Williams, *Sir Walter Raleigh*, 1962; Penguin edition, 1965, pages 84–5):

*Her Majesty and you have placed Sir Walter Raleigh as
Lord Warden of the Stannaries, but amongst so rough and
mutinous a multitude, 10,000 or 12,000, the most strong
men of England, it were meet their governor were one whom
the most part well accounted of, using some familiarity, and
abiding amongst them. Whereas no man is more hated than
him; none cursed more daily by the poor, of whom infinite
numbers are brought to extreme poverty through the gift of
cloth to him. His pride is intolerable, without regard to any,
as the world knows; and as for dwelling amongst them, he
neither does nor means it, having no place of abode; so that
in time of service, this head must either fight without a body,
or else the members will cut off such a head.*

Furthermore, the elections for the consulship in the play
are conducted in exactly the same manner as elections to
the Elizabethan House of Commons; Brutus and Sicinius,
the two Tribunes of the People, are depicted as a pair of
City magistrates; and the Roman mob is drawn from the
London mob that Shakespeare knew. Little more than
thirty years after *Coriolanus* was written, this same mob,
skilfully organized by Pym, exerted a decisive influence on
the trial of Strafford, whom they had been taught to look
on as an enemy of the people. The very language of the
play, describing political opponents as noxious beasts, is
the language of politics at the end of the sixteenth and the
beginning of the seventeenth centuries – and in our own
day. At Raleigh's trial in 1603 Sir Edward Coke, the
Attorney-General, called him a monster and a viper, both
of them words that the Tribunes and Coriolanus hurl at
each other in the central scenes of the play; and, when the
bill of attainder against Strafford was being debated in the
Commons in 1641, the argument was advanced that it was
a waste of time to discuss it, since it had never been

accounted cruel or foul play to knock foxes and wolves on the head. *Coriolanus* is about English as well as Roman politics. The fear the hero expresses when he says (III.1.109–12) that

> *when two authorities are up,*
> *Neither supreme . . . confusion*
> *May enter 'twixt the gap of both and take*
> *The one by th'other*

was to become reality in 1642. In fact, the danger was already becoming clear to some perceptive minds, of which Shakespeare's may well have been one, as early as 1606, when James I was running into trouble with his first Parliament, some of whose members he had described in November 1605 as 'Tribunes of the People, whose mouths could not be stopped'.

Jacobean as well as Roman, *Coriolanus* would certainly have been topical when it was first staged in London around the year 1608, for in 1607 there had been an outbreak of unrest and rioting in Leicestershire, Northamptonshire, and Shakespeare's native Warwickshire. Made desperate by a long period of dearth, the peasantry of these counties pulled down enclosures and began to dig up the land. This revolt of the Diggers or Levellers, as some of the insurgents called themselves, was soon put down, though not without bloodshed. Class feelings seem to have been strongly aroused, and the local gentry took a prominent part in suppressing the peasants.

These events could have been in Shakespeare's mind when he wrote the first scene of his play, showing a riot in Rome, caused by a dearth of corn. They were not, however, its *raison d'être*. It was in North's *Plutarch* that he read of 'Sedition at Rome, by reason of famine' (*Narrative and Dramatic Sources of Shakespeare*, edited by Geoffrey

Bullough, volume v, London and New York, 1964, p. 516, note 1). The origins of *Coriolanus* are to be found in his reading and in the development of his art as a dramatist, rather than in happenings contemporary with its composition. His contact with Plutarch's work was one of the great turning-points in Shakespeare's career. The first result of it in the form of a play, as distinct from passing references, was *Julius Caesar*, written in 1599, which has been aptly described by Granville-Barker as 'the gateway to the tragedies'. Plutarch, who lived from A.D. 46 to a date after 120, was a moralist as well as a historian, and he wrote history in the form of biographies of eminent men. Keenly interested in character – an aspect of his work that probably attracted Shakespeare to it – he is adept at using minute details of personal behaviour, and revealing anecdotes, in order to shed light on the complex psychology of a man. It is these little touches which transform his worthies into individual human beings. His *Parallel Lives* (so called because he treats his heroes in pairs, coupling a Greek and a Roman together and drawing comparisons between them) had been translated into English by Sir Thomas North in 1579 as *The Lives of the Noble Grecians and Romans*, and it was in this translation that Shakespeare knew them. The tragedies that followed *Julius Caesar* were derived from other sources, but after the completion of *Macbeth* in 1605–6 Shakespeare went back to Plutarch once more and used him as the main authority for the last three tragedies that he wrote: *Timon of Athens, Antony and Cleopatra*, and *Coriolanus*.

The connexions between *Timon of Athens* and *Coriolanus* are so close and so striking that it looks rather as though the one play may have grown out of the other. *Timon*, which seems to have been abandoned by its author before he had properly finished it, is, like *Coriolanus*, the story of a man who comes to hate his native city because it has treated him with gross ingratitude. This story is paralleled and reinforced by another, that of Alcibiades, the soldier and statesman who is banished from Athens because he opposes honour and the soldierly values to the usury of the Senate, and who returns leading an avenging army. Plutarch couples Alcibiades with Coriolanus and compares them with each other, showing a decided preference for the Greek, who was much the better politician of the two. What could be more likely, therefore, than that Shakespeare, dissatisfied with what he had made of the stories of Timon and Alcibiades, should have taken up the same basic themes again in the form of a story which lay so ready to his hand as that of Coriolanus? It is also possible that he was attracted to it by the contrast, which is very pronounced in Plutarch's narrative, between the young, austere soldier, in whose life there were only two women – his mother and his wife – and the middle-aged, licentious Antony, the one at the mercy of his own irascibility, and the other of his 'unreined lust of concupiscence', as North puts it. No other two plays in the canon provide a more vivid demonstration of the range and variety of Shakespeare's art than do these, *Antony and Cleopatra* taking the whole extent of the Roman empire as its setting, *Coriolanus* confining itself to the city and its immediate environs: the first exhibiting his prodigality of invention at its height, the second dominated by his searching intelligence.

The *Life* as related by Plutarch is a straightforward piece of biography, beginning with an account of the hero's ancestors and upbringing, and ending with his death. Shakespeare rearranges the events in the service of a dramatic idea. The opposition between Coriolanus and the common people of Rome, which begins to assume importance only about a third of the way through Plutarch's narrative, is placed in the very forefront of the play; within a few lines of the opening the First Citizen describes him as 'chief enemy to the people'. Not many lines later, in the course of an argument with the Second Citizen, the same character accuses him of pride and emphasizes his dependence on his mother. Later in the same scene comes news of the resumption of the war with the Volsces, whereupon the hero expresses his admiration for their leader, Tullus Aufidius, and states his long-standing rivalry with him, a matter that is not mentioned at all in the *Life* until after his banishment has taken place. The scene ends with the two Tribunes, left alone as they will be at the end of so many other scenes in the first half of the play, voicing their dislike and suspicion of him and their determination to watch events carefully. There is already a conspiratorial air about them. The attention of the audience has been focused on issues as well as personalities; the process of converting biography into drama has been carried a long way.

These changes are typical of Shakespeare's manner of working. They are made only when necessary. If the *Life* supplies him with all, or nearly all that he wants, as it does, for example, in the case of Volumnia's appeal to her son in V.3, he takes it over almost word for word with little more alteration than is required to turn prose into blank verse. When it does not, he provides entire scenes of his own invention, such as II.1 and III.2. He also varies the emphasis. Coriolanus's hatred of Rome, after he has been banished from it, is far more intense and indiscriminate in the play than it is in the *Life*. It takes the form of a determination to set fire to the city and destroy it utterly, whereas Plutarch states that he took care that the Volsces under his command spared 'the noblemen's lands and goods', while doing all the harm they could to those of the common people, in order to exacerbate still further the antagonism between the two classes in Rome. The image of the blazing city – itself a projection of the hero's burning resentment – which for Bradley dominates the action as it approaches its climax, is something imported into the original story by Shakespeare. It creates a sense of Coriolanus's implacability, and, therefore, of the extreme danger that Rome is in, which is not present to anything like the same degree in Plutarch.

Another major change of emphasis is of a different kind. In the *Life* the intervention of the women in an effort to save Rome is attributed to divine inspiration. 'Some god' prompts Valeria to go to Volumnia and Virgilia to solicit their aid in an appeal to Coriolanus. In the play the women go to him of their own free will, out of a patriotic desire to preserve the city. There is no hint that they have been moved to do so by any supernatural power. The alteration is deliberate and artistically right, for the whole atmosphere and ambience of *Coriolanus* is secular. Characters may occasionally call on the gods, but there is no sense of the numinous anywhere in it. The interests it arouses and satisfies are political, social and psychological, not religious.

2

The action is organized along direct, massively simple lines. In considering it, the five Acts into which the play is divided in the First Folio are best forgotten. They are unlikely to be Shakespeare's, since there are no Act divisions in those of his plays which appeared in print during his lifetime. Moreover, while the break between Act One and Act Two is necessary, marking as it does the transference of the action from Corioles to Rome, that between Act Two and Act Three is positively misleading, since it indicates a pause at a point where the action is continuous. The basic structure of *Coriolanus* is three movements, preceded by a kind of overture which occupies the first three scenes and introduces all the main characters as well as the leading issues. The first movement, covering the rest of Act One, deals with the war between the Romans and the Volsces. It takes place in and around Corioles. Here, and for the only time in the play, the hero is completely in his element, knowing exactly what he must do and delighting in the exercise of his profession. He infuses something of his own martial ardour into his men and is entirely successful in all that he undertakes. His fortunes reach their height in I.9, where the whole army recognizes his supreme excellence as a soldier and where the title of Coriolanus is bestowed on him as a mark of honour. The second movement, extending from II.1 to IV.2, is the great central section of the play, the most searching piece of political drama that Shakespeare ever wrote. It takes place entirely in Rome, opening with Coriolanus's return to his native city in triumph and ending with his banishment from it with the hoots of the populace sounding in his ears. His apparent success in being chosen consul proves illusory. The two Tribunes, whose weapons are words and chicanery, turn out to be more formidable opponents than the Volsces were. The final movement, subtly preluded by the meeting of a Volsce with a traitor from Rome somewhere between the two territories in IV.3, reproduces the pattern of the second with variations. Instead of entering Rome in triumph, Coriolanus enters Antium as a refugee and in disguise. Nevertheless, he again achieves an apparent success when his desperate gamble of challenging Aufidius's generosity comes off. But this initial advantage only leads to further defeats. First, his mother, by her pleading, forces him to abandon his purpose of destroying Rome;

and then Aufidius, now jealous of his new ally, provokes him into self-assertion with a carefully calculated speech, and secures his assassination.

The structure points to the main concerns of the play. *Coriolanus* is about the relationship between the individual – in this case an exceptional individual of commanding presence, heroic stature, and outstanding ability – and the community. Rome is as much involved in the drama as Coriolanus himself, and it is vividly realized and brought to life in the verse. It is a city pulsating with life and activity, inhabited by a 'multiplying swarm' of people. There are 'tradesmen singing in their shops', magistrates judging petty cases, and citizens yawning in congregations. And, above all, there are crowds. When Coriolanus returns from the wars in II.1, the entire population turns out to welcome him home (lines 202–5).

> *Stalls, bulks, windows*
> *Are smothered up, leads filled, and ridges horsed*
> *With variable complexions, all agreeing*
> *In earnestness to see him.*

There is an obvious and pointed contrast between this anonymous throng and the object of their attentions, who, as even Brutus is constrained to admit, appears almost divine; and the simplest way of viewing the action, though it is not one that commends itself easily or readily to the modern audience or reader, is as a straightforward conflict between black and white, between 'the one', who is noble and brave, and 'the many', who are base and cowardly. The nobility of the hero is insisted on throughout the tragedy. As he enters for the first time Menenius addresses him as 'noble Martius'; as his body is borne off at the end Aufidius says 'he shall have a noble memory'. More than once he is referred to as a god, and he is compared to Her-

cules. Not only is his courage unquestioned and un-
questionable, but he is also a most able general. He takes
Corioles, he converts Cominius's retreat into a successful
attack, and even Aufidius's own servants are forced to
admit that as a leader he is far superior to their master.
Moreover, he is completely free from all the meaner and
more sordid vices. Untouched by covetousness – even the
citizens who loathe him have to grant him this much – he
is also immune to the temptations of ambition. The first
sign of a rift between him and his mother becomes
apparent when he answers to her desire to see him consul
by telling her (II.1.194–6):

> *Know, good mother,*
> *I had rather be their servant in my way*
> *Than sway with them in theirs.*

Regarding himself as a servant of the state, he is not
interested in power for its own sake, and (II.2.125–6)

> *rewards*
> *His deeds with doing them. . . .*

Unlike Aufidius, with whom he has much in common and
who acts as a foil to him, he is not jealous of others, and he
never resorts to base or underhand means. All that the
Elizabethans understood by the word 'policy', meaning the
use of intrigue and deception to secure political ends, is
utterly foreign to his nature. In this respect he compares
favourably not only with the Volscian leader and with the
Tribunes, but also with his own allies and even with his
mother, who, in III.2, asks him to play the part of a
demagogue, to conceal his real feelings and convictions,
and to cajole the people in the manner of Menenius.
Devoted to the ideal of personal honour, steadfast in his
beliefs, and incapable of acting, or telling a lie, Coriolanus

is a man without a mask in a world where hypocrisy and double-dealing hold sway.

The plebeians, and still more their leaders, the two Tribunes, are his absolute antithesis. All that Coriolanus says about them in the first scene is true and is borne out by their subsequent actions. As soldiers they are cowardly and show far more interest in looting than in fighting. As citizens they are completely mutable and untrustworthy, changing their opinions and attitudes on the slightest provocation or inducement. The Tribunes are far worse than the people whom they are supposed to represent. Elected to defend the popular cause, they are concerned solely with retaining, and, if possible, extending, their own personal power. Quite cynical about those who have put them in office, they are ready to lie or to bring false charges in order to achieve their ends. They are envious and mean, always prompt to see motives of self-interest at work when they are confronted, as they are at the end of I.1, by behaviour that is too noble and generous to enter into their scheme of things. Hypocritical, self-seeking, and unprincipled, they have no ideals and no appreciation of the value ideals can have for others, and especially for a man whose whole nature is quite beyond their reach or comprehension.

Nevertheless, at the end of the play, the Tribunes emerge with their power unaffected, and the people, though no better off than they were at first, are at least no worse off either. The victim is Coriolanus, who has been destroyed in the struggle. The man whose 'nature is too noble for the world' has been defeated by the world, which goes on its way unheeding. His downfall is a result not of his faults but of his virtues, of his refusal to seem something other than he is, and of his constitutional inability to suppress the truth that is in him. The tragic sense embodied in his experience is profoundly pessimistic: men in general have no use for, and will not tolerate, disinterested excellence which puts them to shame; their reaction to it is to do all they can to secure its overthrow. And, having the advantage of numbers, they will succeed in their efforts.

This reading of *Coriolanus* has the virtue of placing it firmly as a tragedy, and of bringing out certain qualities in it which are all too easily overlooked in an age that is suspicious of greatness in any form, and particularly so of military greatness. It is, however, inadequate to express the total significance that the play carries, for it can only be arrived at by ignoring the intensely critical light in which the hero is viewed. This is so powerful and so evident that a concentration on it alone can turn the tragedy into a satire. Instead of being a heroic figure, Coriolanus appears from this point of view as the lop-sided and immature product of a faulty education. Emotionally he has never grown up; his dependence on his mother, stressed at the play's opening, remains with him throughout his career, leaving him almost pathetically subject to her dominance. In every conflict between them she forces him into submission by the exercise of her overmastering will. Aufidius's final taunt, when he calls Coriolanus 'thou boy of tears', is all the more unbearable because it is only too true. Incomplete as a man, he is also incomplete as a citizen. Not only does he despise all who are not of his own class, but he does not really care for Rome itself. His talk of his duty towards the state and of his services to it is no more than clap-trap, for, when his professions are put to the test, he is quite ready to destroy the city for the satisfaction of his own personal honour, on which he sets an absurdly high value. His ultimate fate is not tragic at all but a just and fitting end for one who has lived for strife and who is utterly incapable of making any constructive contribution to society.

The fact that two such contrary interpretations of the protagonist can be advanced indicates that the truth is a good deal more complex than either. In fact, Shakespeare himself makes it plain that there can be no simple or ready-made judgement of this particular hero. One of the most marked features of *Coriolanus* is the large number of choric scenes in it. Time after time two people, or two groups of people, come together to discuss Coriolanus's behaviour and character, and on each occasion the pattern of the discussion is the same. Two antithetical views of him are put forward and left unreconciled. Even when this choric function is transferred to a single person, Aufidius, in IV.7, no final conclusion is arrived at. In the last analysis there is something mysterious about him; judgement is baffled. Men are either for him or against him, they cannot regard him with detachment or indifference.

In this respect the treatment of the hero is strikingly similar to the treatment of Roman politics. Shakespeare's presentation of the class struggle is so judicious, and therefore so ambiguous, that it has given the play a peculiar contemporary relevance. During this century Fascists and Communists alike have seized on *Coriolanus* for their own purposes. When it was produced at the Comédie Française in 1934, the invectives of Coriolanus against the Tribunes were so relished by all the anti-democratic cliques that the atmosphere at more than one performance became like that of a turbulent public meeting. More recently Bertolt Brecht, who was fascinated by it, was working on an adaptation and translation of it, designed to give it a Marxist colouring, at the time of his death in 1956. The mere fact that such diverse interpretations of it are even possible endorses the accuracy of Coleridge's judgement that *Coriolanus* 'illustrates the wonderfully philosophic impartiality of Shakespeare's politics'. Impartiality on the part of Shakespeare is, in fact, the very core of the play. It is evident in his depiction of the hero no less than in that of the events in which he is involved. It has to be, for there is no separation of them from each other. *Coriolanus* is the last of the History plays as well as the last of the Tragedies.

3

The connexion between *Coriolanus* and the Histories is particularly clear in Shakespeare's handling of the crowd, or rabble as it is so often called, which has a most important part in the action. He had been interested in it from the outset of his career, when he wrote the scenes dealing with Cade's revolt in *2 Henry VI*. Between that time and the composition of *Coriolanus* he had used it again in *Julius Caesar*. In all three plays his attitude towards it is a consistent one: he makes a clear distinction between men as they are when they are not part of the crowd and what they become when they are caught up in it. Outside the crowd, talking to one another, his citizens are individuals, usually good-humoured, frequently shrewd and sensible, and always distinct from one another. When they are absorbed into it, however, they lose that uniqueness which is the mark of a human being, and are wholly governed by mass emotions, especially by the urge to destroy. A crowd is, therefore, to him a negation of all that makes a man a man; though composed of human beings, it is inhuman, unnatural, and monstrous, a threat to all civilized living.

A city, on the other hand, is a natural thing. In an Elizabethan translation of Aristotle's *Politics*, made by a certain 'I.D.' and published in 1598, which almost certainly influenced Shakespeare's thinking when he was writing *Coriolanus*, it is defined thus:

23

*A city is a perfect and absolute assembly or communion of many towns or streets in one, having already attained to the highest pitch of perfection and self-sufficiency, and being ordained not only to this end to live, but also to live well. And seeing that the former simple societies have their beginning from nature, therefore also a city doth subsist by nature.*

Being a natural association of men, the city-state is like a man and can be described and understood in terms of the human body. This idea, which still survives in such phrases as 'the body politic', is put forward in the very first scene of the play when Menenius tells the mutinous citizens the fable of the belly. The fable is in Plutarch's *Life*, but Shakespeare also knew it from many other sources, because it was one of the great commonplaces of the time, so well known that the First Citizen has no difficulty at all in picking up its implications and trying to turn them against Menenius. 'A.B.' makes use of the same analogy in his letter to Burghley, quoted at p. 11. It is a concrete expression of the Elizabethan conception of the state as an ordered whole in which each class and occupation had its separate place, or degree as it was called, in the hierarchy. As a theory of government it insisted on the need for subordination. The task of the upper classes was to rule; the duty of the lower classes was to obey, in the same way that the limbs carry out orders from the brain. As a theory of society, however, it insisted on the importance of the community and on the dependence of men on one another, because, as the Elizabethan Homily of Obedience says, 'every one have need of other'. Each section of society had its own specific function to perform and was necessary to the well-being of the whole. In return, it was entitled to its fair, as distinct from equal, reward in the form of worldly goods.

Shakespeare's whole way of thinking about human problems was dominated by the idea of Nature and the natural, and he seems to have accepted the theory in its entirety, but to have become increasingly critical of the way in which it could be and was being abused and ignored in his time. Nowhere does he suggest that the ordinary citizen has any right to take part in the business of government. As well might one expect the foot to take over the work of the head. The only possible result would be confusion and chaos. But he is also emphatic that all men, different though their degrees may be, are nevertheless members of the community and that each has his rights. One of the main themes of *King Lear* is the perversion of authority into oppression which first makes, and then ignores, 'houseless poverty'. In Shakespeare's eyes the right to rule carries with it responsibility for the welfare of the ruled. It is his neglect of this essential duty that comes home to Lear on the heath and makes him cry out, 'O, I have ta'en too little care of this.' It is a necessary condition of health in the state that power should be exercised justly for the benefit of the community as a whole and not of any one class or section of it.

At the opening of *Coriolanus*, Rome, the social organism, is sick; and its illness, which is frequently referred to in terms of images drawn from the practice of medicine and surgery, grows worse as the play goes on. The citizens' main complaint – and it is obviously not a groundless one – is that they are not being treated as human beings at all. They are starving, but the patricians, who have plenty of grain, will do nothing to relieve their distress. Menenius's tale expounding how the state ought to function is not an answer to their grievances but a device to fob them off. He cynically uses the ideal of the interdependent community as a political weapon, without really believing in it, just as he cleverly gives the citizens the impression that he regards them as fellow-men by addressing them as 'my good friends, mine honest neighbours'. His true attitude appears when, having pacified them with his diplomacy, he is at last in a position to say what he thinks, and says it in no uncertain terms (lines 160–61):

> *Rome and her rats are at the point of battle;*
> *The one side must have bale.*

Rome he identifies with himself and his class. The ordinary citizens are not fellow-men, members of the same body politic, but vermin.

Rome, as it is depicted at the beginning of the play, is not a community at all in the full sense of the word; and before the first scene is over, this breakdown in human relations has already had bad political consequences. Denied the elementary rights that are their due, the plebeians seek to take part in the business of government, which is not their legitimate sphere of activity. In doing so they deliver themselves into the hands of demagogues who aim at personal power. The body politic has become a divided thing; it has no integrity or wholeness. The two groups into which it has split regard each other with the hatred engendered by incomprehension. 'What's the matter?', the first words that Coriolanus speaks to the citizens, is a question that will be repeated time and again as the play goes on. It is hardly ever a genuine request for information, still less does it voice concern: it is normally a cry of exasperation. Each group sees the other as inhuman. The First Citizen describes Coriolanus as 'a very dog to the commonalty', while he, in turn, addresses the crowd as 'you curs'. And, because each side denies the humanity of the other, there is no respect for life. The First Citizen's remedy for the people's distress is futile and dangerous:

'Caius Martius is chief enemy to the people . . . Let us kill him, and we'll have corn at our own price.' Coriolanus's prescription for the ills of Rome is equally futile and even more frightening, because it is so indiscriminate and uttered with such evident relish (lines 195–8):

> *Would the nobility lay aside their ruth*
> *And let me use my sword, I'd make a quarry*
> *With thousands of these quartered slaves as high*
> *As I could pick my lance.*

Characteristically he is saying precisely what he thinks. One of his most striking qualities is his absolute honesty. It is his strength and his weakness. To him the riot is a mutiny to be put down by force. He takes the soldier's dangerously over-simplified view of a complex problem in civil life. Strongly aware of the need for authority in the state, he is quite oblivious of the equal need for social justice, and utterly incapable of realizing the intimate connexion between the two things. Clear-sighted in one way – he recognizes at once the risks inherent in the appointment of tribunes – he is blind in another. What he says about the fickleness of the crowd is perfectly true; but his manner of saying it is aggressive and provocative, while his attitude to their sufferings is callous. In his eyes they have no rights whatever, not even to life itself. Assuming that there can be no possible relationship between himself and them, he regrets that he has not been allowed to hunt them as though they were wild animals, and greets the news of the forthcoming war with the Volsces as a heaven-sent opportunity to thin down the excess population. It is clear also from the language he uses that he feels he has far more in common with Aufidius, his opposite number in the Volscian camp, than he has with the plebeians of his own city.

Coriolanus is a divided being. Like Rome itself, he lacks wholeness. His integrity is limited to honesty; it does not include completeness as a man. The analogy between the individual and the state works both ways. Man is a little kingdom, just as the state is a large man; and in this little kingdom reason should rule. In Coriolanus it does not; he is dominated by passions, and above all by anger and impatience. Over-developed on one side of his nature, he is under-developed and stunted on the other. This dichotomy is hinted at in some of the first words said about him. When the Second Citizen argues that he has done great services for Rome, the First retorts (I.1.35–7):

> *Though soft-conscienced men can be content to say it was for his country, he did it to please his mother and to be partly proud. . . .*

Pride suggests self-sufficiency and independence, but the desire to please his mother suggests their opposites. Coriolanus is a compound of contrarieties, some of them rooted in his own nature but others of his mother's making. It is from her, as he states at the opening of III.2, that he has learnt to despise the common people and to take his right to rule over them for granted, without any consideration for their welfare. She has, in fact, done much to shape his life, and the main function of I.3 is to show how she did it. There she tells Virgilia that she set the pursuit of honour and distinction in battle before him as the only worthwhile goal in life, and expresses her own preference for the war-like virtues as against the values of love and procreation. It becomes evident too that she also encouraged him to be brutal in the belief that it was manly. When Valeria relates how she has seen Coriolanus's little son tearing a harmless butterfly to pieces in a sudden fit of temper, Volumnia remarks (I.3.67) with considerable complacency, 'One on's father's moods.' Coriolanus has been taught to repress all manifestations of tenderness. At the same time he has discovered that success in war is the way to his mother's love and approval. As a result he has never grown up emotionally. He is an extreme case of what E. M. Forster calls the 'undeveloped heart'. By refusing to acknowledge his need for love, he is completely at the mercy of that need. The absolute contrast to him in this respect is his wife Virgilia, the 'gracious silence' at the heart of this stormy play, who is all love and tenderness, and, in being so, often excites the scorn of her Amazonian mother-in-law. Yet Virgilia, because she does acknowledge her own feelings and is not afraid of them, can stand up to Volumnia as Coriolanus cannot. In this same revealing scene she quietly sticks by her determination not to go out, despite the rather vulgar pressure that Volumnia and Valeria bring to bear on her.

A further consequence of the hero's unfortunate up-bringing is that he simply does not understand the meaning of the words 'kind', 'kindly', and 'kindness', which are fundamental to Shakespeare's conception of the organic human society. 'Kind' is related to 'kin'. Kindness is first the feeling that the child has for the mother from whose breast it is nourished. Thence the bond is extended to the family and, ultimately, to the community at large, to humankind. It is, therefore, the basis of society; without it, men could not live together. In the election scene, II.3, Coriolanus mockingly asks one of the citizens, 'your price o'th'consulship?', and receives the answer, 'The price is to ask it kindly.' His reply is to use the word sarcastically. From his mother he has sucked the spirit of contention rather than 'the milk of human kindness', and, as a result, that extension of feeling which ought to take place in the individual as he grows up has not happened to him. Even his wife comes second to his mother in his affections. Furthermore, this frustration of the primal emotions has left his patriotism flawed. The full complex of relationships involved is stated by Cominius in III.3 when, after the sentence of banishment has been passed on Coriolanus, he makes a last effort to induce the Tribunes to think again. He says (lines 111–15):

> *I do love*
> *My country's good with a respect more tender,*
> *More holy and profound, than mine own life,*
> *My dear wife's estimate, her womb's increase*
> *And treasure of my loins.*

Coriolanus thinks of himself as a servant of the state, but Rome has never taken on this kind of emotional reality for him.

Volumnia's training has made her son a formidable soldier, but not a happy warrior. The admiration excited by his achievements in the battle scenes is qualified by criticism. His unaided entry into Corioles is magnificent in its daring, and his success in fighting his way out again inspires the rest to emulate him and capture the town. But the lustre of the deed is somewhat dimmed by his cursing of the soldiers who gave way earlier in the same scene, behaviour which is obviously meant to be contrasted with Cominius's more generous and encouraging words to his troops when they are forced to retire at the opening of I.6. For the frailties of the common soldier, Coriolanus has nothing but a searing contempt. The only time that he feels a true sense of comradeship with others is when he calls for volunteers, later in I.6, and *'They all shout and wave their swords'*. Fired by his words, they have accepted his cult of honour. He has for the moment made them his.

Transported out of himself with joy, he offers his body to them as a weapon:

> *O' me alone, make you a sword of me.*

It is the one occasion in the play when he feels completely at one with a group of other men.

It is revealing that at this point he should think of himself as a sword, for a whole series of images referring to him suggest that there is something of the war machine about him. Imagining his activities, Volumnia, in I.3, sees him as a harvest-man, mowing down all before him; and the same impression of impersonal force is created by the words with which she heralds his return to Rome (II.1.153-4):

> *Death, that dark spirit, in's nervy arm doth lie,*
> *Which, being advanced, declines, and then men die.*

Cominius's epic speech in praise of him in the next scene is full of similar images; and they crop up again, though this time with an ironic effect, since, unknown to the user of them, Coriolanus has relented in his purpose, when, in V.4, Menenius is describing his inflexibility to Sicinius. They emphasize his valour, but they also imply that the price of military efficiency, such as he displays, is a certain loss of humanity.

The images through which his nobility is conveyed also have an ambiguous undertone. At various times he is referred to by others as a bear, a dragon, an osprey, and a tiger, while he compares himself to a dragon at one point and to an eagle at another. All these are creatures that men tend to think of as noble and that have a heraldic significance, but they are also birds and beasts of prey. Furthermore, he himself is much given to seeing others in animal terms. He thinks of Aufidius as a lion, and of the plebeians as dogs, hares, geese, the herd, and so on. These images are not in general unpleasant or repulsive, but their repeated use by him and about him does have the effect of creating an impression of his difference from other men and of his remoteness from them, which Plutarch calls his 'solitariness'. It is reinforced by a number of other references to him of a very different kind. They begin when Brutus tells Sicinius, in II.1, of the great reception Coriolanus has received at his homecoming. He calls it (lines 210–13):

> *Such a pother*
> *As if that whatsoever god who leads him*
> *Were slily crept into his human powers*
> *And gave him graceful posture.*

From this point onwards Coriolanus is often spoken of as though he were a god, and in IV.5 Aufidius actually addresses him as 'thou Mars'. Later in the scene the Third Servingman says that he is being treated by the Volscian leaders 'as if he were son and heir to Mars', as, indeed, in a way he is, since this is the meaning of his name Martius.

Man's proper place in the creation, according to the most generally accepted ideas in Shakespeare's time, was midway between the animals, to which he was related by his mortal body and his senses, and the angelic or divine order of being, with which he shared an immortal soul and the gift of reason. Like Timon, to whom Apemantus can say with justice (*Timon of Athens*, IV.3.299–300), 'The middle of humanity thou never knewest, but the extremity of both ends', Coriolanus swings in an unbalanced way to either end of the scale, instead of remaining poised at the centre of it. The dangers attaching to this instability are concisely expressed by Aristotle in the *Politics* (I.2), where he writes: 'He that is incapable of living in society is a god or a beast.' *Coriolanus* is a demonstration of its corollary.

32

The hero, welcomed back to Rome as though he were divine, proves incapable of living in society, and is driven out of the city as though he were a wild beast.

Yet his attitude to the people who banish him has not changed in the interval between these two events. What has changed is the name they give to him. The saviour of his country has become a traitor and an enemy to the people. The central movement of the play is a terrifying exhibition of the power of words. Speech is, as Ben Jonson says in his *Discoveries*, 'the instrument of society', because without it the intercourse of man and man, which is essential for civilized living, is impossible. But its use is fraught with dangers, for words can make things seem other than they are, and alter the significance or the importance of an action entirely, as Aufidius points out at the end of IV.7 when he says (lines 49–50):

> *So our virtues*
> *Lie in th'interpretation of the time. . . .*

Coriolanus is a victim of words, of what he says and of what is said about him. He is half aware of the danger, for in II.2 he tells Brutus (line 70):

> *When blows have made me stay, I fled from words.*

But he cannot restrain his own tongue, and scorns making any attempt to do so. His response to anything that touches his honour or stings his pride is instinctive, immediate, and devoid of all caution.

Coriolanus's vulnerability to words is connected with his failure as a human being. He cannot converse with other men, for conversation implies reciprocity, and there can be no reciprocity for one who refuses to admit his relationship with others. Behind this deficiency, at a deeper level still, lies his inability to come to terms with the needs and weaknesses of his own nature. Intensely self-conscious, he has no powers of introspection, and, consequently, no self-knowledge. The feeling of solidarity with a group that he experiences in I.6 does not last. As soon as the battle is over, he withdraws into isolation, rejecting, with a self-depreciating modesty that is an extreme form of pride, the generous praise Cominius gives him. Avid of fame, he cannot bear the thought that anyone should suspect him guilty of 'that last infirmity of noble mind'. When his fellow-soldiers cheer him for refusing an extra share of the spoils, he roundly accuses them of flattery. Similar conduct mars the triumph of his homecoming. Public acclamations offend his heart; Cominius's eulogy of him in II.2 he never hears at all, having left his place in the Senate House before Cominius begins to speak, in order to avoid listening to it. His concern is with himself and his personal dignity at a time when the most important office in the state is about to be bestowed on him. The Senate offers it to him as a reward for his services, and he accepts it as such with no realization that it involves responsibilities other than military ones.

Shakespeare's great contemporary, Richard Hooker, had written in 1593 (*Of the Laws of Ecclesiastical Polity*, I. ix. 12) that all government rests ultimately on the consent of the governed:

> *because, although there be according to the opinion of some very great and judicious men, a kind of natural right in the noble, wise, and virtuous, to govern them which are of servile disposition; nevertheless for manifestation of this their right, and men's more peaceable contentment on both sides, the assent of them who are governed seemeth necessary.*

This need for a demonstration of the consent of the

governed is recognized in the Rome of the play by the time-honoured custom of the candidate for the consulship appearing before the people to ask for their votes, clad in a 'gown of humility' as a mark of his kinship with them and of his dependence on them. Noble and virtuous but far from wise, Coriolanus has no understanding of the custom's significance. He can only see it as it affects his self-respect and the honour on which he so prides himself. He finds it intolerable on three counts: it is a pointless and unnecessary charade, since he already has the voice of the Senate, who are the ruling class; it involves begging for something that is his by right of birth and service; worst of all, it will mean putting on an act, pretending to be what he is not and cannot be. Putting personal considerations first, he asks to be released from complying with the custom. The self-styled defender of the established order is quite ready to overturn it when it demands something that runs counter to his own will and dignity. The central conflict of the play has begun. Already at odds with the people, he now finds himself at odds with his own class, for the Senate disregards his plea. More important still, he is at odds with himself, torn between his desire that his excellence be recognized and his instinctive aversion from doing anything that smacks of insincerity or flattery, which will lower him in his own esteem.

His way out of this dilemma is something of a subterfuge. He decides to save his honour by turning the election into a palpable farce. There will be no false pretences. He will ask the citizens for their votes in a manner that will make it abundantly plain that he despises them, and that he regards their 'voices' as so much 'stinking breath'. But he has not reckoned with the fact that one aspect of their mutability is a readiness to forget the past, and that, as Menenius remarks in III.2.88–9:

> *they have pardons, being asked, as free*
> *As words to little purpose.*

Good-humoured, slow of wit and determined to be fair, they miss the full meaning of his biting ironies and sarcastic jeers. Puzzled and bewildered, rather than affronted or insulted, they give him their votes, and in doing so add to his sense that he has cheapened himself. At the practical level, his elaborate attempt to be honest has merely provided the Tribunes with exactly the situation they can exploit.

Brutus and Sicinius are consummate politicians. They know the ways of the world as Coriolanus does not, and they have no scruples about playing a part. Seeing him – quite rightly from their point of view – as a threat to their newly-won authority, they determine to 'break his neck' before he breaks theirs. Their handling of the people at the end of the election scene is a classic exposure of the methods of the demagogue, and recalls Antony's management of the crowd in the second Forum scene in *Julius Caesar*. Swiftly and efficiently the citizens' perplexed frustration at Coriolanus's rejection of their efforts to be fair and generous is transformed into a passionate and violent resentment. The men who at the scene's opening talked sensibly and responsibly about their duties as citizens have by the end of it ceased to be individuals at all. They have become – to use two images that occur in the next scene – a river in flood bearing all down before it (III.1.247–9), and a Hydra, the many-headed monster of Greek myth (III.1.93).

In the third Act the tensions and strains, which have been increasing from the beginning, reach breaking-point. Rome is divided against itself, and so is the hero. Having enraged the people, the Tribunes proceed to enrage him. It is easy enough. Sicinius's first words to him are a command: 'Pass no further', and it is followed by a series of other commands, culminating in the most provocative of imperatives, 'shall', and in the accusation, which is all the more galling because there is so much truth in it (III.1. 80–82):

> You speak o'th'people
> As if you were a god to punish, not
> A man of their infirmity.

These challenges destroy any vestiges of restraint in him. Ignoring the cautions of Menenius and the First Senator, he gives way to his choler, expressing his innermost thoughts and feelings with no regard whatever for the consequences. His strength and his weakness, inextricably entangled with each other, are revealed in his central speech when he says (lines 142–9):

> This double worship,
> Where one part does disdain with cause, the other
> Insult without all reason; where gentry, title, wisdom,
> Cannot conclude but by the yea and no
> Of general ignorance – it must omit
> Real necessities, and give way the while
> To unstable slightness. Purpose so barred, it follows
> Nothing is done to purpose.

It is a marvellously accurate definition of the consequences of faction. The turbulent activity within the state prevents all effective action by the state. But Coriolanus lays the entire responsibility for the ills that afflict Rome on one party alone: the plebeians, whom he thinks of as a diseased limb infecting the body politic. His remedy, which even he admits to be a dangerous one, is to resort to surgery: 'at once pluck out | The multitudinous tongue'. To achieve

unity he proposes action that may well lead to civil war,
and he does it in words which vividly recall his stirring
appeal for volunteers in I.6. It is an attempt (IV.7.43-5)
at

> *commanding peace*
> *Even with the same austerity and garb*
> *As he controlled the war. . . .*

It demonstrates his fatal inflexibility of temper, and it does
not work. His fellow patricians – as he is soon to discover –
do not share his conception of nobility or his absolute
refusal to temporize.

His advocacy of force gives the initiative to the Tribunes,
and they take full advantage of it. Heedless of any ultimate
consequences, they fan the flames of popular fury. Their
cure for the sickness of the city is exactly the same as his;
they order his death (III.1.219-21, saying to Menenius,
who counsels caution and temperance):

> *Sir, those cold ways,*
> *That seem like prudent helps, are very poisonous*
> *Where the disease is violent.*

Coriolanus is saved for the moment by his courage and by
the help of his friends, but not before fighting has broken
out. In the last part of the scene, where Menenius tries to
reason with the Tribunes, the whole argument turns on
whether the hero is an incurable disease in the body
politic that must be cut away, or whether he is, as Menenius
says:

> *a limb that has but a disease –*
> *Mortal, to cut it off; to cure it, easy.*

The words illustrate perfectly the intimate connexion
Shakespeare establishes in this play between the public and

the private worlds, and the way in which the instability of the protagonist and the instability of the state exacerbate each other.

So far Coriolanus has kept his integrity of spirit. His conduct has been rash, unstatesmanlike and provocative, but it has been all of a piece. Now comes the decisive test. In the first lines of III.2 he proclaims his determination to continue on his course and defy the plebeians, no matter what the consequences to him. The consequences to Rome do not enter into his thoughts. But there are unexpected difficulties: his mother no longer approves of his actions, though what he has done and is doing is the logical outcome of her teaching. As she enters he asks her:

> *Why did you wish me milder? Would you have me*
> *False to my nature?*

The answer is that she would. To Volumnia the fulfilling of her ambitions for her son is more important than any principles. The honour she has held up before him proves to be a tainted thing. She advises him to practise lying and dissimulation, to cultivate the art of flattery, which he has always so despised, in order to recover the power he is in such danger of losing. There is, in fact, nothing to choose between her and the Tribunes; like them she is an exponent of policy. In her eyes the end justifies the means. She asks him to tell a lie, to go to the people (lines 55–7)

> *with such words that are but roted in*
> *Your tongue, though but bastards and syllables*
> *Of no allowance to your bosom's truth.*

And she actually gives him a practical demonstration of the act that he must put on.

This is the real crisis of the play. Coriolanus can either remain loyal to his own code – which, narrow and rigid though it is, is the only consistent value held by any character, apart from Virgilia – or he can betray it. Everything is at stake here; not only his self-respect, but also his chance of ever living a truly independent life of his own, free from Volumnia's dominance. He feels an instinctive revulsion against her counsel, but he finds difficulty in putting it into words. His replies are brief and petulant, rather than argued and coherent. And then she puts on the pressure, backed up by Menenius and even by the soldierly Cominius. She asserts her naked will, adds cajolery to it, and then resorts to emotional bullying. It is too much for her son. He has just said (lines 120–23):

> *I will not do't,*
> *Lest I surcease to honour mine own truth*
> *And by my body's action teach my mind*
> *A most inherent baseness.*

'Inherent' means fixed and ineradicable; he knows that by lending himself to deception he will do himself irreparable damage. But his mother is the one emotional loyalty of his life. Compared with this, his cult of honour, his loyalty to class and state are nothing. Unable to understand why he gives way, he nevertheless submits out of the blind but compelling need to have her approval. From this moment he is lost. Having betrayed himself, he is bound to go on to other betrayals. The rest of the play is implicit in this scene. Now that the basic principle of his life, his integrity, has been destroyed, he is like some tremendous force without an object, erratic and dangerous, because utterly at the mercy of passions he does not understand.

Even from the patricians' point of view his self-betrayal accomplishes nothing. When he returns to the market-place, he finds, as he knew he would, that he cannot act the part of a prostitute and a mountebank. He never really has a chance to, for the Tribunes are the producers. They have arranged beforehand for the people to behave like a stage army, and they have decided on their tactics: they will 'put him to choler straight'. It is all cheap, nasty, and effective. The word 'traitor' which infuriated him in III.1 has the same result here. His sense of honour and of his own worth and achievement is stung to the quick. All thoughts of his promise to his mother forgotten, he utters scathing and defiant speeches of contempt. It is the classic situation of epic poetry: the one standing against the many, supported only by his pride and courage. And it wins admiration; the many are so petty and mean, and the one so magnificent in his refusal to be cowed by them or to submit. But the admiration is not unqualified. The proper pride that a man should feel in being himself and standing up for the faith that is in him, no matter what the odds, is transformed into something else when Coriolanus turns on the people who have banished him, to tell them 'I banish you!' It is not only unrealistic, it is also the manifestation of a pride that has gone beyond its proper limits and become a towering egotism. His unwillingness to admit to any kind of relationship with other men has brought him to this pass; yet he has learnt nothing from the experience. He seems to think that he can live without them far more easily than they can live without him. It is manifestly untrue. There is also an element of the absurd about it, for he has been manoeuvred into this position by a couple of old men, as though he were a pawn on a chess-board. In this respect Coriolanus is curiously like the people he scorns. Both they and he can be manipulated by the clever and the unscrupulous, because they are so deficient in self-knowledge.

The effects of Coriolanus's betrayal of himself are not immediately apparent. His bearing in defeat contrasts favourably with his reactions to success, and adds much to his tragic stature. To his mother, his wife, and his friends he is considerate and kindly, not vicious in a rather futile manner as Volumnia is when she curses the citizens. He seems resigned and even hopeful, speaking of his future with dignity and assurance (IV.1.51–3):

> *While I remain above the ground you shall*
> *Hear from me still, and never of me aught*
> *But what is like me formerly.*

As he takes his farewell there is only one hint of what is to come. It is conveyed through an image that condenses pride and self-sufficiency on the one hand, and a devastating sense of isolation and desolation on the other, into a single complex feeling (IV.1.29–31):

> *I go alone,*
> *Like to a lonely dragon that his fen*
> *Makes feared and talked of more than seen. . . .*

When he next appears he is almost unrecognizable. He is, as the graphic stage direction puts it, *'in mean apparel, disguised and muffled'*. The change in his appearance corresponds to a change in him. He has felt the full effect of what are for Shakespeare two of the bitterest experiences life can bring: banishment and ingratitude. From *Romeo and Juliet*, on through *Richard II*, and so to Kent in *King Lear* and Alcibiades in *Timon of Athens*, the pain of exile is felt time after time as one of the worst things that can happen to a man; it is a severing of the roots by which he lives. Similarly, the suffering caused by the ingratitude of others echoes through *As You Like It*, *King Lear*, and *Timon of Athens*.

Indeed, the two actions are closely linked with each other in Shakespeare's mind; both are unnatural, and are likely to produce unnatural reactions in the minds of those who suffer them. Cut off from the society which, much as he scorned many of its members, was nevertheless his home, Coriolanus is a lost man seeking for his identity. The dereliction that he feels, and expresses in his bearing, is caught by Aufidius when he says to him (IV.5.64–5):

> *Though thy tackle's torn,*
> *Thou show'st a noble vessel.*

The soliloquy he utters as he stands outside Aufidius's house is unlike anything he has said in the play hitherto, apart from his one previous soliloquy of self-disgust in the middle of the election scene. The man who prided himself on his integrity now takes the line that there is no such thing, and that human relationships are made and unmade by chance. There is no solid basis for either hatred or friendship; everything hangs on 'Some trick not worth an egg'. The cynicism that pervades the speech is an attempt to rationalize and justify the blind resentment that has led him to Antium. But behind it there lies something deeper which emerges when he says (IV.4.23–4):

> *My birthplace hate I, and my love's upon*
> *This enemy town.*

The statement is paradoxical and completely unnatural. Coriolanus is trying to turn the whole frame of things, including himself, upside down in an effort to establish some connexion, if only the negative one of hostility, between himself and Rome. He feels he is 'a kind of nothing, titleless' until (V.1.14–15) he has

> *forged himself a name i'th'fire*
> *Of burning Rome.*

In fact, he is striking an attitude. He knows and admits

43

to Aufidius that his basic motive is 'mere spite', something unworthy of him, but, sustained by pride and his sense of injured merit, he attempts the impossible, and seeks to stand (V.3.36–7)

> *As if a man were author of himself*
> *And knew no other kin.*

The situation in which he speaks these words emphasizes their unreality. Even as they are uttered, his mother, his wife, and his son are standing before him, and he is feeling the pull of affection and instinct, of all the bonds and ties which for Shakespeare are summed up in the one word, Nature. There have been clear indications already that he knows he is acting a part in his repeated calls to Aufidius to notice his constancy. Now he admits it to himself. When Virgilia speaks to him he says (lines 40–42):

> *Like a dull actor now*
> *I have forgot my part and I am out,*
> *Even to a full disgrace.*

The monstrosity of his position is further brought home to him by Volumnia's kneeling before him, which he recognizes as a total perversion of all the sanctities of his life. Nevertheless, his pride does not surrender readily to the compulsions of 'Great Nature', and he tries to forestall his mother's most powerful argument by saying to her before she begins her plea:

> *Tell me not*
> *Wherein I seem unnatural.*

She has to exert all her powers of persuasion to win him over. But this time her speech is free from policy. In III.2 she asked him to be untrue to himself and to act a dishonourable role; now she asks him to be true to himself and to abandon the false part he is playing. The very centre of her plea is that he should be 'honest' with himself, and he finds it irresistible. When it comes to the test – and it is the most positive and attractive of all his qualities, that which makes him a tragic hero – Coriolanus always tells the truth. She has demonstrated to him the necessary connexions between 'honesty' and 'honour', between his relationship to his own family and his relationship to Rome, 'The country, our dear nurse'. He admits the truth of the demonstration.

But there are other features of Volumnia's 'oration' that also help to sway him. In the first place, she herself has changed. The values she sets before him now are more feminine than any she has paid service to before. Words like 'grace', 'reconcile', 'mercy', 'peace' and 'fellowship' come unexpectedly from her lips, but they are sincerely meant. Volumnia has learnt something in the interval since IV.2, where she prided herself on her anger and rebuked Virgilia for weeping. She has at last seen the truth of what her daughter-in-law has stood for all along. Secondly, however, she appeals to the future which is there before him in the form of his son, born, as Virgilia says:

> to keep your name
> Living to time.

Fame has always mattered to him, and her version of the verdict of history on his action if he perseveres in his intended course is a most telling argument.

Exactly what goes on in Coriolanus while his mother is speaking has to be deduced from the way in which he has steeled himself against her before she begins, and then from what he does, rather than from what he says, since he is allowed only one brief speech in the course of nearly a hundred lines. It is, however, enough to bring out the

intensity of the conflict within him, for it is combined with
two highly significant actions. He rises from his seat with
the words (lines 129–31):

> *Not of a woman's tenderness to be*
> *Requires nor child nor woman's face to see.*
> *I have sat too long.*

But, although he gets up, he does not go away; and at the
end of Volumnia's appeal there comes the most eloquent
of all Shakespeare's stage directions: '*Holds her by the
hand, silent*'. It is a moment of pure drama. The positive
values the play embodies are presented in visual form.
Nature has triumphed over the monstrous. The struggle
between self-sufficiency and the need for relationship is
finished. Coriolanus's pride is broken. The great potential
for life that has hitherto lain suppressed in him is at last
revealed. One realizes what he might have been had he
struck a fairer balance between the claims of honour and
the claims of Virgilia.

As it is, in realizing himself he destroys himself. He can
only be honest with his mother at the price of being dis-
honest with the Volsces and breaking an oath which he
should never have taken. With that paradoxical logic that
operates in the world of tragic experience he is caught in a
trap of his own contriving. In one of those flashes of insight
that are so often vouchsafed to the tragic hero in moments
such as this, he realizes his danger and abandons himself
to his fate, telling Volumnia (V.3.187–90):

> *You have won a happy victory to Rome.*
> *But for your son – believe it, O believe it –*
> *Most dangerously you have with him prevailed,*
> *If not most mortal to him. But let it come.*

The moment passes, however, and he seems to delude

himself into the belief that he can satisfy the Volsces with what he has achieved already. But he reckons without Aufidius, who is a cheaper version of himself, and whose essential meanness of spirit throws his own nobility up in high relief. Aufidius manipulates him exactly as the Tribunes did. Once again the word 'traitor' does its work. For the last time he asserts his own singleness of being, recalling his feats in Corioles and flaunting his name like a challenge. He has recovered his lost identity. Isolated from Rome, he becomes wholly Roman again. His final action reunites him with his native city. The Volscian crowd, which shortly before hailed his return, turn on him as the Roman crowd did. He is killed and trodden on. It is the fate he has been moving towards ever since the play's beginning, his inevitable and predestined end, a thing so logically and artistically right that it is felt almost as a consummation.

In this final movement of the drama Rome receives less attention, but it is not forgotten. Nicanor, the Roman traitor who appears in IV.3, relates that Coriolanus's exile has not ended the class struggle; on the contrary, 'the nobles . . . are in a ripe aptness to take all power from the people and to pluck from them their tribunes for ever'. Nor does the first news of his defection to the enemy serve to heal the wound in the body politic. In IV.6 Cominius and Menenius take a positive delight in laying the blame for what has happened on the Tribunes. But by V.1 war has had a unifying effect. Cominius has already been to plead with Coriolanus, and the Tribunes seek to persuade Menenius to see what he can do. They are genuinely concerned for Rome, and are not held back by any false pride. Moreover, they are now aware of values that meant nothing to them before; they speak of love and kindness. At the end of the scene they go with Cominius to make their 'fair

47

entreaties' to the ladies. By attacking Rome, Coriolanus has done far more to bring the factions together than he ever did while he lived in it. At the same time there is no facile optimism about Shakespeare's final picture of the city. The crowd is as mutable as ever, ready at one moment to tear the Tribunes to pieces, at the next to repeal Coriolanus's banishment and to cheer his mother and wife into the gates.

Often described as a bleak play, because the hero's faults and weaknesses are analysed with an accuracy that makes any kind of identification with him difficult and well-nigh impossible, *Coriolanus* is, in fact, an affirmation of the values of honesty, kindness, and relationship, and of the fundamental importance of 'the human heart by which we live'. It faces squarely the difficulties of living together that confront all communities, and it asserts the validity of natural ties, of what Wordsworth calls (*The Prelude*, II.243–4) – writing of the child –

> *The gravitation and the filial bond*
> *Of nature that connects him with the world.*

# FURTHER READING

(1) *Editions and Editorial Problems*

THE most recent scholarly edition (to which the present editor owes a considerable debt) is by J. Dover Wilson in *The New Shakespeare*, Cambridge, 1960. Some useful guidance on difficult and controversial passages in the play will be found in *New Readings in Shakespeare*, by C. J. Sisson, Cambridge, 1956.

(2) *Sources*

The handiest and most accessible version of the main source of the play, Sir Thomas North's translation of Plutarch's *The Life of Martius Coriolanus*, is in *Shakespeare's Plutarch*, edited by T. J. B. Spencer, Penguin Books, Harmondsworth, 1964. Other material which Shakespeare may have used, together with an illuminating survey of the way in which he modified and dramatized it all, is available in *Narrative and Dramatic Sources of Shakespeare*, edited by Geoffrey Bullough, volume v, London and New York, 1964. There is a brief but valuable account of Shakespeare's treatment of the matter at his disposal in *Shakespeare's Sources*, by Kenneth Muir, volume I, reprinted with new appendices, London, 1961.

(3) *Criticism*

Matters of fundamental importance for the understanding and interpretation of *Coriolanus* were first raised in the early nineteenth century. In his *Characters of Shakespear's Plays*, published in 1817, Hazlitt expressed the view that in this particular play Shakespeare revealed his own political attitudes, showing that he 'had a leaning to the arbitrary side of the question . . . and . . . spared no occasion of baiting the rabble'. A year later, Coleridge in his *Notes and Lectures upon Shakespeare*, which were not published until 1849, came out with precisely the opposite opinion, when he said, 'This play illustrates the wonderfully philosophic impartiality of Shakespeare's politics.' The debate thus initiated is still unfinished. Most modern critics are in agreement with Coleridge, but Hazlitt has received some support from J. Middleton Murry in an essay entitled 'A Neglected Heroine of Shakespeare', originally written in 1921 and subsequently republished in *Countries of the Mind*, London, 1931, and also from W. H. Clemen in the chapter he devotes to the play in his book, *The Development of Shakespeare's Imagery*, London, 1951.

There is an extended and detailed discussion of *Coriolanus* in M. W. MacCallum's *Shakespeare's Roman Plays and Their Background*, London, 1910, but while much that is said there is sensible and acceptable, especially the section on Shakespeare's use of Plutarch, the total result is not very exciting. Much more enlightening is A. C. Bradley's British Academy Lecture of 1912, published in *A Miscellany*, London, 1929, because it asks questions that are of permanent interest. Comparing *Coriolanus* with the plays that had been the subject of his *Shakespearean Tragedy*, Bradley finds it lacking in imaginative extension and in inward conflict. A radically different assessment of the play in relation to the tragedies that had preceded it was suggested by T. S. Eliot in his essay on *Hamlet*, first published in 1919, where it is seen as 'Shakespeare's most assured artistic success'. Bradley, however, has had his supporters. His view of *Coriolanus* is substantially shared by Granville-Barker in his *Preface* to the play, first published in 1947, which has some good things to say about problems of production, but is otherwise rather disappointing. Much more valuable is John Palmer's consideration of the play in his *Political Characters of Shakespeare*, London, 1945. Ignoring the fact that *Coriolanus* is a poetic drama, Palmer treats it rather as though it were an actual political event of the 1930s, and produces one of the few defences of the Tribunes that have been made. Coriolanus himself he characterizes, somewhat sweepingly, as a 'splendid oaf'.

The things that Palmer omits from his essay are precisely

those that G. Wilson Knight concentrates on in his brilliant treatment of the play in *The Imperial Theme*, London, 1931, where he shows that the distinctive style of *Coriolanus* is essential to its total significance and to the presentation of the hero. His insights lead on to and are complemented by the more moralistic approach of L. C. Knights, who has insisted repeatedly and convincingly on the relevance of the tragedy, as a piece of political wisdom, for our own time, and for all times. His essays dealing with it are most conveniently accessible in *Some Shakespearean Themes*, London, 1959, and in *Further Explorations*, London, 1965. In his conviction that the dominant tone of the play is critical, Knights had been anticipated by D. A. Traversi in *An Approach to Shakespeare*, London, 1938 (revised and enlarged, 1957), and by F. N. Lees in his important article 'Coriolanus, Aristotle and Bacon', published in *The Review of English Studies*, 1950. Further support for this view comes from Willard Farnham in his book *Shakespeare's Tragic Frontier*, Berkeley and Los Angeles, 1950, and from D. J. Enright in his essay '*Coriolanus*: Tragedy or Debate?', published in *Essays in Criticism*, 1954. This last drew a spirited and effective rejoinder from I. R. Browning, who argues in '*Coriolanus*: Boy of Tears' (*Essays in Criticism*, 1955) that the hero, though subject to criticism, is nevertheless a genuinely tragic figure. Similar conclusions are reached by Hermann Heuer, who emphasizes the element of the mysterious in the play, in his article 'From Plutarch to Shakespeare: A Study of Coriolanus' (*Shakespeare Survey 10*, 1957). Also on the same side, though he works from a very different set of assumptions, is E. M. Waith, who puts forward the idea that modern criticism of the play has tended to belittle the hero because it has failed to recognize him as a specific type of which the Renaissance strongly approved (*The Herculean Hero*, London, 1962).

Finally, there are two recent treatments of the play that bring out its paradoxical qualities: Maurice Charney's *Shakespeare's Roman Plays*, Harvard University Press, 1961, the most thorough analysis of the imagery that has yet been made; and D. J. Gordon's subtle and closely argued essay 'Name and Fame:

Shakespeare's Coriolanus', published in *Papers Mainly Shakespearian*, edited by G. I. Duthie, Edinburgh and London, 1964, which relates the discussion of 'honour' in this play to similar discussions in *1 Henry IV* and *Troilus and Cressida*. The contradictory impulses in the hero, and their underlying causes, are also sympathetically dealt with by Una Ellis-Fermor in 'Coriolanus', published in *'Shakespeare the Dramatist' and Other Papers by Una Ellis-Fermor*, edited by Kenneth Muir, London, 1961.

# THE LANGUAGE OF THE PLAY

THE richness and vitality of Shakespeare's plays is due in no small measure to the fact that they were written at a time when the English language was developing at a rate never equalled before or since. In *Coriolanus* this trend is most obvious in the speech of Menenius, who coins words almost as he needs them, but it is also evident in such linguistic blunders as that of the Third Servingman at IV.5.215, when he speaks of 'directitude' without having any idea of what he really means by this, to him, imposing term. One consequence of this rapid growth is that many of the words used by Shakespeare have now become obsolete or have disappeared entirely from modern English. (These, however, cause no difficulty to the reader of the present day, since he will naturally look them up in the Commentary.) The real stumbling-block is the appearance in his writings of many other words which are still a familiar part of the English we speak, but which no longer mean to us what they meant to him, or which had in his day an additional meaning to that which they have now. These can be extremely misleading, and it therefore seems desirable to give a list of some of the most common of them occurring in *Coriolanus*.

*abuse* deceive, mislead
*affect* desire, aim at
*affection* inclination, desire
*attend* await
*but* except
*come off* retire (military)
*comfortable* cheerful
*determine* terminate, end
*discover* reveal, show
*discovery* revelation

*hardly* with difficulty
*owe* own, possess
*passing* surpassingly, extremely
*present* immediate
*presently* immediately, at once
*press a power* raise an army
*pretence* intention, design
*sensible* sensitive, feeling
*still* always, constantly
*success* outcome, result

An additional difficulty in this particular play is an extensive use in it, as in *Antony and Cleopatra*, of shortened and colloquial forms. At first sight somewhat disconcerting to the modern reader, because of their unfamiliarity, these forms are soon accepted and, indeed, appreciated for their effect in helping to give the play that rapid and impetuous quality which is one of its most striking characteristics. The most important of them are the following:

| | | | |
|---|---|---|---|
| *'a* | he | *on's* | of his, of its |
| *an't* | if it | *on't* | of it |
| *'has* | he has | *o'th'* | of the |
| *in's* | in his, in its | *to th'* | to the |
| *i'th'* | in the | *y'are* | ye are |

# CORIOLANUS

# THE CHARACTERS IN THE PLAY

CAIUS MARTIUS, afterwards Caius Martius Coriolanus
TITUS LARTIUS ⎫
COMINIUS ⎭ Roman generals against the Volsces
MENENIUS AGRIPPA, friend of Coriolanus
SICINIUS VELUTUS ⎫ Tribunes of the People, opposed
JUNIUS BRUTUS ⎭ to Coriolanus
A Crowd of Roman Citizens
A Roman Herald
NICANOR, a Roman in the pay of the Volsces

VOLUMNIA, mother of Coriolanus
VIRGILIA, wife of Coriolanus
YOUNG MARTIUS, son of Coriolanus
VALERIA, friend of Virgilia
A Gentlewoman attending on Virgilia

TULLUS AUFIDIUS, General of the Volsces
A Lieutenant under Aufidius
Conspirators with Aufidius
ADRIAN, a Volsce
A Citizen of Antium
Two Volscian Guards

Roman and Volscian Senators, Patricians, Aediles, Lictors, Soldiers, Messengers, Volscian Citizens, Servants of Aufidius, and other Attendants

*Enter a company of mutinous Citizens, with staves,*
*clubs, and other weapons*

FIRST CITIZEN Before we proceed any further, hear me
  speak.

ALL Speak, speak.

FIRST CITIZEN You are all resolved rather to die than to
  famish?

ALL Resolved, resolved.

FIRST CITIZEN First, you know Caius Martius is chief
  enemy to the people.

ALL We know't, we know't.

FIRST CITIZEN Let us kill him, and we'll have corn at   10
  our own price. Is't a verdict?

ALL No more talking on't. Let it be done. Away, away!

SECOND CITIZEN One word, good citizens.

FIRST CITIZEN We are accounted poor citizens, the patricians good. What authority surfeits on would relieve
  us. If they would yield us but the superfluity while it
  were wholesome, we might guess they relieved us
  humanely. But they think we are too dear. The leanness
  that afflicts us, the object of our misery, is as an inven-
  tory to particularize their abundance. Our sufferance is a   20
  gain to them. Let us revenge this with our pikes ere we
  become rakes. For the gods know I speak this in hunger
  for bread, not in thirst for revenge.

SECOND CITIZEN Would you proceed especially against
  Caius Martius?

FIRST CITIZEN Against him first. He's a very dog to the
  commonalty.

59

SECOND CITIZEN Consider you what services he has
done for his country?

30 FIRST CITIZEN Very well, and could be content to give
him good report for't, but that he pays himself with being
proud.

SECOND CITIZEN Nay, but speak not maliciously.

FIRST CITIZEN I say unto you, what he hath done
famously he did it to that end. Though soft-conscienced
men can be content to say it was for his country, he did
it to please his mother and to be partly proud, which he
is, even to the altitude of his virtue.

SECOND CITIZEN What he cannot help in his nature you
40 account a vice in him. You must in no way say he is
covetous.

FIRST CITIZEN If I must not, I need not be barren of
accusations. He hath faults, with surplus, to tire in repetition.

*Shouts within*

What shouts are these? The other side o'th'city is risen.
Why stay we prating here? To th'Capitol!

ALL Come, come.

FIRST CITIZEN Soft, who comes here?

*Enter Menenius Agrippa*

SECOND CITIZEN Worthy Menenius Agrippa, one that
50 hath always loved the people.

FIRST CITIZEN He's one honest enough. Would all the
rest were so!

MENENIUS

What work's, my countrymen, in hand? Where go you
With bats and clubs? The matter? Speak, I pray you.

FIRST CITIZEN Our business is not unknown to th'
Senate. They have had inkling this fortnight what we
intend to do, which now we'll show 'em in deeds. They
say poor suitors have strong breaths. They shall know
we have strong arms too.

MENENIUS

Why, masters, my good friends, mine honest neighbours,   60
Will you undo yourselves?

FIRST CITIZEN

We cannot, sir, we are undone already.

MENENIUS

I tell you, friends, most charitable care
Have the patricians of you. For your wants,
Your suffering in this dearth, you may as well
Strike at the heaven with your staves as lift them
Against the Roman state, whose course will on
The way it takes, cracking ten thousand curbs
Of more strong link asunder than can ever
Appear in your impediment. For the dearth,   70
The gods, not the patricians, make it, and
Your knees to them, not arms, must help. Alack,
You are transported by calamity
Thither where more attends you, and you slander
The helms o'th'state, who care for you like fathers,
When you curse them as enemies.

FIRST CITIZEN Care for us? True indeed! They ne'er
cared for us yet. Suffer us to famish, and their store-
houses crammed with grain; make edicts for usury, to
support usurers; repeal daily any wholesome act estab-   80
lished against the rich, and provide more piercing
statutes daily to chain up and restrain the poor. If the
wars eat us not up, they will; and there's all the love they
bear us.

MENENIUS

Either you must
Confess yourselves wondrous malicious,
Or be accused of folly. I shall tell you
A pretty tale. It may be you have heard it,
But, since it serves my purpose, I will venture
To stale't a little more.   90

**FIRST CITIZEN** Well, I'll hear it, sir. Yet you must not
think to fob off our disgrace with a tale. But, an't please
you, deliver.

**MENENIUS**

There was a time when all the body's members
Rebelled against the belly, thus accused it:
That only like a gulf it did remain
I'th'midst o'th'body, idle and unactive,
Still cupboarding the viand, never bearing
Like labour with the rest, where th'other instruments
Did see and hear, devise, instruct, walk, feel,
And, mutually participate, did minister
Unto the appetite and affection common
Of the whole body. The belly answered –

**FIRST CITIZEN**

Well, sir, what answer made the belly?

**MENENIUS**

Sir, I shall tell you. With a kind of smile,
Which ne'er came from the lungs, but even thus –
For look you, I may make the belly smile
As well as speak – it tauntingly replied
To th'discontented members, the mutinous parts
That envied his receipt; even so most fitly
As you malign our senators for that
They are not such as you.

**FIRST CITIZEN**                     Your belly's answer – What?
The kingly crownèd head, the vigilant eye,
The counsellor heart, the arm our soldier,
Our steed the leg, the tongue our trumpeter,
With other muniments and petty helps
In this our fabric, if that they –

**MENENIUS**                             What then?
'Fore me, this fellow speaks! What then? What
then?

FIRST CITIZEN

Should by the cormorant belly be restrained
Who is the sink o'th'body –

MENENIUS                    Well, what then?                    120

FIRST CITIZEN

The former agents, if they did complain,
What could the belly answer?

MENENIUS                    I will tell you.

If you'll bestow a small – of what you have little –
Patience awhile, you'st hear the belly's answer.

FIRST CITIZEN

Y'are long about it.

MENENIUS                    Note me this, good friend –

Your most grave belly was deliberate,
Not rash like his accusers, and thus answered.
'True is it, my incorporate friends,' quoth he,
'That I receive the general food at first
Which you do live upon; and fit it is,                    130
Because I am the storehouse and the shop
Of the whole body. But, if you do remember,
I send it through the rivers of your blood
Even to the court, the heart, to th'seat o'th'brain;
And, through the cranks and offices of man,
The strongest nerves and small inferior veins
From me receive that natural competency
Whereby they live. And though that all at once' –
You, my good friends, this says the belly, mark me –

FIRST CITIZEN

Ay, sir, well, well.

MENENIUS                    'Though all at once cannot                    140

See what I do deliver out to each,
Yet I can make my audit up, that all
From me do back receive the flour of all,
And leave me but the bran.' What say you to't?

**FIRST CITIZEN**

It was an answer. How apply you this?

**MENENIUS**

The senators of Rome are this good belly,
And you the mutinous members. For examine
Their counsels and their cares, digest things rightly
Touching the weal o'th'common, you shall find
150   No public benefit which you receive
But it proceeds or comes from them to you,
And no way from yourselves. What do you think,
You, the great toe of this assembly?

**FIRST CITIZEN**

I the great toe? Why the great toe?

**MENENIUS**

For that being one o'th'lowest, basest, poorest
Of this most wise rebellion, thou goest foremost.
Thou rascal, that art worst in blood to run,
Lead'st first to win some vantage.
But make you ready your stiff bats and clubs.
160   Rome and her rats are at the point of battle;
The one side must have bale.

    *Enter Caius Martius*     Hail, noble Martius!

**MARTIUS**

Thanks. What's the matter, you dissentious rogues,
That rubbing the poor itch of your opinion
Make yourselves scabs?

**FIRST CITIZEN**     We have ever your good word.

**MARTIUS**

He that will give good words to thee will flatter
Beneath abhorring. What would you have, you curs,
That like nor peace nor war? The one affrights you,
The other makes you proud. He that trusts to you,
Where he should find you lions, finds you hares;
170   Where foxes, geese. You are no surer, no,

Than is the coal of fire upon the ice
Or hailstone in the sun. Your virtue is
To make him worthy whose offence subdues him
And curse that justice did it. Who deserves greatness
Deserves your hate; and your affections are
A sick man's appetite, who desires most that
Which would increase his evil. He that depends
Upon your favours swims with fins of lead
And hews down oaks with rushes. Hang ye! Trust ye?
With every minute you do change a mind                    180
And call him noble that was now your hate,
Him vile that was your garland. What's the matter
That in these several places of the city
You cry against the noble Senate, who,
Under the gods, keep you in awe, which else
Would feed on one another? What's their seeking?

MENENIUS

For corn at their own rates, whereof they say
The city is well stored.

MARTIUS                    Hang 'em! They say?
They'll sit by th'fire and presume to know
What's done i'th'Capitol, who's like to rise,                    190
Who thrives and who declines; side factions and give out
Conjectural marriages, making parties strong
And feebling such as stand not in their liking
Below their cobbled shoes. They say there's grain
        enough!
Would the nobility lay aside their ruth
And let me use my sword, I'd make a quarry
With thousands of these quartered slaves as high
As I could pick my lance.

MENENIUS

Nay, these are almost thoroughly persuaded,
For though abundantly they lack discretion,                    200

65

Yet are they passing cowardly. But, I beseech you,
What says the other troop?

MARTIUS                    They are dissolved. Hang 'em!
They said they were an-hungry, sighed forth proverbs –
That hunger broke stone walls, that dogs must eat,
That meat was made for mouths, that the gods sent not
Corn for the rich men only. With these shreds
They vented their complainings; which being answered
And a petition granted them – a strange one,
To break the heart of generosity
210 And make bold power look pale – they threw their caps
As they would hang them on the horns o'th'moon,
Shouting their emulation.

MENENIUS                    What is granted them?

MARTIUS

Five tribunes to defend their vulgar wisdoms,
Of their own choice. One's Junius Brutus, one
Sicinius Velutus, and – I know not. 'Sdeath!
The rabble should have first unroofed the city
Ere so prevailed with me. It will in time
Win upon power and throw forth greater themes
For insurrection's arguing.

MENENIUS                    This is strange.

MARTIUS
220 Go get you home, you fragments.

> *Enter a Messenger, hastily*

MESSENGER
Where's Caius Martius?

MARTIUS                    Here. What's the matter?

MESSENGER
The news is, sir, the Volsces are in arms.

MARTIUS
I am glad on't. Then we shall ha' means to vent
Our musty superfluity. See, our best elders.

*Enter Cominius, Titus Lartius, with other Senators;*
*Junius Brutus and Sicinius Velutus*

FIRST SENATOR
　Martius, 'tis true that you have lately told us:
　The Volsces are in arms.

MARTIUS　　　　　　　　They have a leader,
　Tullus Aufidius, that will put you to't.
　I sin in envying his nobility,
　And were I anything but what I am,
　I would wish me only he.

COMINIUS　　　　　　　You have fought together.　230

MARTIUS
　Were half to half the world by th'ears and he
　Upon my party, I'd revolt, to make
　Only my wars with him. He is a lion
　That I am proud to hunt.

FIRST SENATOR　　　　Then, worthy Martius,
　Attend upon Cominius to these wars.

COMINIUS
　It is your former promise.

MARTIUS　　　　　　　Sir, it is,
　And I am constant. Titus Lartius, thou
　Shalt see me once more strike at Tullus' face.
　What, art thou stiff? Stand'st out?

LARTIUS　　　　　　　No, Caius Martius,
　I'll lean upon one crutch and fight with t'other　240
　Ere stay behind this business.

MENENIUS　　　　　　　O, true bred!

FIRST SENATOR
　Your company to th'Capitol, where I know
　Our greatest friends attend us.

LARTIUS (*to Cominius*)　　　Lead you on.
　(*to Martius*) Follow Cominius. We must follow you.
　Right worthy you priority.

67

COMINIUS                                        Noble Martius!

FIRST SENATOR (*to the Citizens*)

    Hence to your homes, be gone.

MARTIUS                                    Nay, let them follow.

    The Volsces have much corn. Take these rats thither

    To gnaw their garners. (*Citizens steal away*) Worshipful

        mutineers,

    Your valour puts well forth. Pray follow.

        *Exeunt Patricians. Sicinius and Brutus stay behind*

SICINIUS

250   Was ever man so proud as is this Martius?

BRUTUS

    He has no equal.

SICINIUS

    When we were chosen tribunes for the people –

BRUTUS

    Marked you his lip and eyes?

SICINIUS                              Nay, but his taunts.

BRUTUS

    Being moved, he will not spare to gird the gods.

SICINIUS

    Bemock the modest moon.

BRUTUS

    The present wars devour him; he is grown

    Too proud to be so valiant.

SICINIUS                              Such a nature,

    Tickled with good success, disdains the shadow

    Which he treads on at noon. But I do wonder

260   His insolence can brook to be commanded

    Under Cominius.

BRUTUS                              Fame, at the which he aims –

    In whom already he's well graced – cannot

    Better be held nor more attained than by

    A place below the first; for what miscarries

Shall be the general's fault, though he perform
To th'utmost of a man, and giddy censure *the public's criticism*
Will then cry out of Martius, 'O, if he
Had borne the business!'

SICINIUS                              Besides, if things go well,
Opinion, that so sticks on Martius, shall
Of his demerits rob Cominius.

BRUTUS                              Come.                              270
Half all Cominius' honours are to Martius,
Though Martius earned them not; and all his faults
To Martius shall be honours, though indeed
In aught he merit not.

SICINIUS                    Let's hence and hear
How the dispatch is made, and in what fashion,
More than his singularity, he goes
Upon this present action.

BRUTUS                    Let's along.                    *Exeunt*


*Enter Tullus Aufidius, with Senators of Corioles*                    I.2

FIRST SENATOR
So, your opinion is, Aufidius,
That they of Rome are entered in our counsels
And know how we proceed.

AUFIDIUS                    Is it not yours?
What ever have been thought on in this state
That could be brought to bodily act ere Rome
Had circumvention? 'Tis not four days gone
Since I heard thence. These are the words – I think
I have the letter here; yes, here it is:

*They have pressed a power, but it is not known* *raised an army*
*Whether for east or west. The dearth is great,*                    10
*The people mutinous. And it is rumoured,*
*Cominius, Martius your old enemy,*

69

Who is of Rome worse hated than of you,
And Titus Lartius, a most valiant Roman,
These three lead on this preparation
Whither 'tis bent. Most likely 'tis for you.
Consider of it.

FIRST SENATOR Our army's in the field.
We never yet made doubt but Rome was ready
To answer us.

AUFIDIUS                    Nor did you think it folly
20  To keep your great pretences veiled till when
They needs must show themselves, which in the hatching,
It seemed, appeared to Rome. By the discovery
We shall be shortened in our aim, which was
To take in many towns ere almost Rome
Should know we were afoot.

SECOND SENATOR                Noble Aufidius,
Take your commission, hie you to your bands.
Let us alone to guard Corioles.
If they set down before's, for the remove
Bring up your army. But, I think, you'll find
30  Th' have not prepared for us.

AUFIDIUS                          O, doubt not that.
I speak from certainties. Nay, more,
Some parcels of their power are forth already,
And only hitherward. I leave your honours.
If we and Caius Martius chance to meet,
'Tis sworn between us we shall ever strike
Till one can do no more.

ALL                           The gods assist you!

AUFIDIUS
And keep your honours safe!

FIRST SENATOR              Farewell.

SECOND SENATOR                      Farewell.

ALL Farewell.                               *Exeunt*

70

*Enter Volumnia and Virgilia, mother and wife to*
*Martius. They set them down on two low stools and sew*

VOLUMNIA I pray you, daughter, sing, or express yourself
in a more comfortable sort. If my son were my husband,
I should freelier rejoice in that absence wherein he won
honour than in the embracements of his bed where he
would show most love. When yet he was but tender-
bodied and the only son of my womb, when youth with
comeliness plucked all gaze his way, when for a day of
kings' entreaties a mother should not sell him an hour
from her beholding, I, considering how honour would
become such a person – that it was no better than pic-   10
ture-like to hang by th'wall, if renown made it not stir –
was pleased to let him seek danger where he was like to
find fame. To a cruel war I sent him, from whence he
returned his brows bound with oak. I tell thee, daughter,
I sprang not more in joy at first hearing he was a man-
child than now in first seeing he had proved himself a
man.

VIRGILIA But had he died in the business, madam, how
then?

VOLUMNIA Then his good report should have been my   20
son; I therein would have found issue. Hear me profess
sincerely, had I a dozen sons, each in my love alike, and
none less dear than thine and my good Martius, I had
rather had eleven die nobly for their country than one
voluptuously surfeit out of action.

*Enter a Gentlewoman*

GENTLEWOMAN Madam, the Lady Valeria is come to
visit you.

VIRGILIA
Beseech you, give me leave to retire myself.

VOLUMNIA
Indeed you shall not.

*even here I hear your husband's army*

30 Methinks I hear hither your husband's drum;
See him pluck Aufidius down by th'hair;
As children from a bear, the Volsces shunning him.
Methinks I see him stamp thus, and call thus:
'Come on, you cowards! You were got in fear,
Though you were born in Rome.' His bloody brow
With his mailed hand then wiping, forth he goes,
Like to a harvest-man that's tasked to mow
Or all or lose his hire.

VIRGILIA
His bloody brow? O Jupiter, no blood!

VOLUMNIA
40 Away, you fool! It more becomes a man
Than gilt his trophy. *monument* The breasts of Hecuba,
When she did suckle Hector, looked not lovelier
Than Hector's forehead when it spit forth blood
At Grecian sword, contemning. Tell Valeria
We are fit to bid her welcome. *Exit Gentlewoman*

VIRGILIA
Heavens bless my lord from fell *dire* Aufidius!

VOLUMNIA
He'll beat Aufidius' head below his knee } *dramatic irony*
And tread upon his neck.
*Enter Valeria, with an Usher and a Gentlewoman*
VALERIA My ladies both, good day to you.
50 VOLUMNIA Sweet madam!
VIRGILIA I am glad to see your ladyship.
VALERIA How do you both? You are manifest housekeep- *plainly* *indoor type*
ers. What are you sewing here? A fine spot, in good faith.
How does your little son?
VIRGILIA I thank your ladyship. Well, good madam.
VOLUMNIA He had rather see the swords and hear a drum *learn* *take up war*
than look upon his schoolmaster.
VALERIA O'my word, the father's son! I'll swear 'tis a

72

very pretty boy. O'my troth, I looked upon him o'Wed-
nesday half an hour together. 'Has such a confirmed 60
countenance! I saw him run after a gilded butterfly, and
when he caught it, he let it go again, and after it again,
and over and over he comes and up again, catched it
again; or whether his fall enraged him, or how 'twas, he
did so set his teeth and tear it. O, I warrant, how he
mammocked it!

VOLUMNIA One on's father's moods.

VALERIA Indeed, la, 'tis a noble child.

VIRGILIA A crack, madam.

VALERIA Come, lay aside your stitchery. I must have you 70
play the idle housewife with me this afternoon.

VIRGILIA No, good madam, I will not out of doors.

VALERIA Not out of doors?

VOLUMNIA She shall, she shall.

VIRGILIA Indeed, no, by your patience. I'll not over the
threshold till my lord return from the wars.

VALERIA Fie, you confine yourself most unreasonably.
Come, you must go visit the good lady that lies in.

VIRGILIA I will wish her speedy strength and visit her
with my prayers, but I cannot go thither. 80

VOLUMNIA Why, I pray you?

VIRGILIA 'Tis not to save labour, nor that I want love.

VALERIA You would be another Penelope. Yet they say
all the yarn she spun in Ulysses' absence did but fill
Ithaca full of moths. Come, I would your cambric were
sensible as your finger, that you might leave pricking it
for pity. Come, you shall go with us.

VIRGILIA No, good madam, pardon me, indeed I will not
forth.

VALERIA In truth, la, go with me, and I'll tell you excel- 90
lent news of your husband.

VIRGILIA O, good madam, there can be none yet.

VALERIA Verily I do not jest with you. There came news
from him last night.

VIRGILIA Indeed, madam?

VALERIA In earnest, it's true. I heard a senator speak it.
Thus it is: the Volsces have an army forth, against whom
Cominius the general is gone with one part of our
Roman power. Your lord and Titus Lartius are set
100 down before their city Corioles. They nothing doubt
prevailing and to make it brief wars. This is true, on
mine honour, and so, I pray, go with us.

VIRGILIA Give me excuse, good madam, I will obey you
in everything hereafter.

VOLUMNIA Let her alone, lady. As she is now, she will
but disease our better mirth.

VALERIA In troth, I think she would. Fare you well, then.
Come, good sweet lady. Prithee, Virgilia, turn thy
solemnness out o'door and go along with us.

110 VIRGILIA No, at a word, madam. Indeed I must not. I
wish you much mirth.

VALERIA Well then, farewell.                    *Exeunt*

I.4                *Enter Martius, Titus Lartius, with Drum and*
                  *Colours, with Captains and Soldiers, as before the city*
                  *Corioles. To them a Messenger*

MARTIUS
Yonder comes news. A wager they have met.

LARTIUS
My horse to yours, no.

MARTIUS                         'Tis done.

LARTIUS                                   Agreed.

MARTIUS
Say, has our general met the enemy?

74

MESSENGER

They lie in view, but have not spoke as yet.

LARTIUS

So, the good horse is mine.

MARTIUS                    I'll buy him of you.

LARTIUS

No, I'll nor sell nor give him. Lend you him I will
For half a hundred years. (*To the trumpeter*) Summon
    the town.

MARTIUS

How far off lie these armies?

MESSENGER                    Within this mile and half.

MARTIUS

Then shall we hear their 'larum, and they ours.
Now Mars, I prithee, make us quick in work,                    10
That we with smoking swords may march from hence
To help our fielded friends! Come, blow thy blast.
    *They sound a parley*
    *Enter two Senators, with others, on the walls of*
    *Corioles*
Tullus Aufidius, is he within your walls?

FIRST SENATOR

No, nor a man that fears you less than he:
That's lesser than a little. (*Drum afar off*) Hark, our
    drums
Are bringing forth our youth. We'll break our walls
Rather than they shall pound us up. Our gates,
Which yet seem shut, we have but pinned with rushes;
They'll open of themselves. (*Alarum far off*) Hark you,
    far off!
There is Aufidius. List what work he makes                    20
Amongst your cloven army.

MARTIUS                    O, they are at it!

75

**LARTIUS**

Their noise be our instruction. Ladders, ho!

*Enter the army of the Volsces*

**MARTIUS**

They fear us not, but issue forth their city.
Now put your shields before your hearts, and fight
With hearts more proof than shields. Advance, brave
      Titus.
They do disdain us much beyond our thoughts,
Which makes me sweat with wrath. Come on, my fellows.
He that retires, I'll take him for a Volsce,
And he shall feel mine edge.

*Alarum. The Romans are beat back to their trenches.*
*Enter Martius, cursing*

**MARTIUS**

30 All the contagion of the south light on you,
You shames of Rome! You herd of – Boils and plagues
Plaster you o'er, that you may be abhorred
Farther than seen, and one infect another
Against the wind a mile! You souls of geese
That bear the shapes of men, how have you run
From slaves that apes would beat! Pluto and hell!
All hurt behind! Backs red, and faces pale
With flight and agued fear! Mend and charge home,
Or, by the fires of heaven, I'll leave the foe
40 And make my wars on you. Look to't. Come on!
If you'll stand fast, we'll beat them to their wives,
As they us to our trenches. Follow's!

*Another alarum. The Volsces fly, and Martius follows*
*them to the gates, and is shut in*

So, now the gates are ope. Now prove good seconds.
'Tis for the followers fortune widens them,
Not for the fliers. Mark me, and do the like.

*He enters the gates*

76

FIRST SOLDIER Fool-hardiness, not I.

SECOND SOLDIER Nor I.

FIRST SOLDIER See, they have shut him in.

ALL To th'pot, I warrant him.

> *Alarum continues*
> *Enter Titus Lartius*

LARTIUS

What is become of Martius?

ALL                           Slain, sir, doubtless.            50

FIRST SOLDIER

Following the fliers at the very heels,
With them he enters, who upon the sudden
Clapped to their gates. He is himself alone,
To answer all the city.

LARTIUS                    O noble fellow!

Who sensibly outdares his senseless sword,
And when it bows stand'st up. Thou art lost, Martius.
A carbuncle entire, as big as thou art,
Were not so rich a jewel. Thou wast a soldier
Even to Cato's wish, not fierce and terrible
Only in strokes, but with thy grim looks and        60
The thunder-like percussion of thy sounds
Thou mad'st thine enemies shake, as if the world
Were feverous and did tremble.

> *Enter Martius, bleeding, assaulted by the enemy*

FIRST SOLDIER                    Look, sir.

LARTIUS                              O, 'tis Martius!

Let's fetch him off, or make remain alike.

> *They fight, and all enter the city*

> *Enter certain Romans, with spoils*            I.5

FIRST ROMAN This will I carry to Rome.

SECOND ROMAN And I this.

THIRD ROMAN A murrain on't! I took this for silver.

*Alarum continues still afar off*
*Enter Martius and Titus Lartius, with a Trumpeter*

MARTIUS
See here these movers that do prize their hours
At a cracked drachma. Cushions, leaden spoons,
Irons of a doit, doublets that hangmen would
Bury with those that wore them, these base slaves,
Ere yet the fight be done, pack up. Down with them!

*Exeunt spoilers*

And hark, what noise the general makes! To him!
10 There is the man of my soul's hate, Aufidius,
Piercing our Romans. Then, valiant Titus, take
Convenient numbers to make good the city,
Whilst I, with those that have the spirit, will haste
To help Cominius.

LARTIUS                Worthy sir, thou bleed'st.
Thy exercise hath been too violent
For a second course of fight.

MARTIUS                        Sir, praise me not.
My work hath not yet warmed me. Fare you well.
The blood I drop is rather physical
Than dangerous to me. To Aufidius thus
20 I will appear and fight.

LARTIUS                Now the fair goddess Fortune
Fall deep in love with thee, and her great charms
Misguide thy opposers' swords! Bold gentleman,
Prosperity be thy page!

MARTIUS                Thy friend no less
Than those she placeth highest. So farewell.

LARTIUS
Thou worthiest Martius.                *Exit Martius*
Go sound thy trumpet in the market-place.
Call thither all the officers o'th'town,
Where they shall know our mind. Away!        *Exeunt*

COMINIUS

Breathe you, my friends. Well fought! We are come off
Like Romans, neither foolish in our stands
Nor cowardly in retire. Believe me, sirs,
We shall be charged again. Whiles we have struck,
By interims and conveying gusts we have heard
The charges of our friends. The Roman gods
Lead their successes as we wish our own,
That both our powers, with smiling fronts encountering,
May give you thankful sacrifice!

*Enter a Messenger*                     Thy news?

MESSENGER

The citizens of Corioles have issued                 10
And given to Lartius and to Martius battle.
I saw our party to their trenches driven,
And then I came away.

COMINIUS                     Though thou speak'st truth,
Methinks thou speak'st not well. How long is't since?

MESSENGER

Above an hour, my lord.

COMINIUS

'Tis not a mile; briefly we heard their drums.
How couldst thou in a mile confound an hour,
And bring thy news so late?

MESSENGER                         Spies of the Volsces
Held me in chase, that I was forced to wheel
Three or four miles about, else had I, sir,                 20
Half an hour since brought my report.

*Enter Martius*

COMINIUS                             Who's yonder
That does appear as he were flayed? O gods!
He has the stamp of Martius, and I have
Before-time seen him thus.

MARTIUS (*shouts*)                    Come I too late?

COMINIUS

The shepherd knows not thunder from a tabor                    *small drum*
More than I know the sound of Martius' tongue
From every meaner man.

MARTIUS                    Come I too late?

COMINIUS

Ay, if you come not in the blood of others,
But mantled in your own.

MARTIUS                    O, let me clip ye
30    In arms as sound as when I wooed, in heart
As merry as when our nuptial day was done,
And tapers burned to bedward!

COMINIUS                    Flower of warriors,
How is't with Titus Lartius?

MARTIUS

As with a man busied about decrees:
Condemning some to death and some to exile,
Ransoming him or pitying, threatening th'other;
Holding Corioles in the name of Rome
Even like a fawning greyhound in the leash,
To let him slip at will.

COMINIUS                    Where is that slave
40    Which told me they had beat you to your trenches?
Where is he? Call him hither.

MARTIUS                    Let him alone.
He did inform the truth – but for our gentlemen.
The common file – a plague! Tribunes for them! –    *flinch*
The mouse ne'er shunned the cat as they did budge
From rascals worse than they.

*great
regard
for
truth*

COMINIUS                    But how prevailed you?

MARTIUS

Will the time serve to tell? I do not think.
Where is the enemy? Are you lords o'th'field?    *victors*

80

If not, why cease you till you are so? *are you "hanging about"*

COMINIUS                      Martius,
We have at disadvantage fought, and did
Retire to win our purpose.                     50

MARTIUS
How lies their battle? Know you on which side
They have placed their men of trust? *best men*

COMINIUS              As I guess, Martius,
Their bands i'th'vaward are the Antiates, *at the front* *capital of the Volsceans*
Of their best trust; o'er them Aufidius,
Their very heart of hope.

MARTIUS               I do beseech you
By all the battles wherein we have fought,
By th'blood we have shed together, by th'vows
We have made to endure friends, that you directly
Set me against Aufidius and his Antiates,
And that you not delay the present, but,         60
Filling the air with swords advanced and darts,
We prove this very hour.

COMINIUS            Though I could wish
You were conducted to a gentle bath *shows military honour*
And balms applied to you, yet dare I never
Deny your asking. Take your choice of those
That best can aid your action.

MARTIUS              Those are they
That most are willing. If any such be here –
As it were sin to doubt – that love this painting *blood as a sign of honour*
Wherein you see me smeared; if any fear
Lesser his person than an ill report;          70
If any think brave death outweighs bad life
And that his country's dearer than himself;
Let him alone, or so many so minded,
Wave thus to express his disposition,
And follow Martius.

>*They all shout and wave their swords, take him up in
their arms, and cast up their caps*

O'me alone, make you a sword of me.
If these shows be not outward, which of you
But is four Volsces? None of you but is
Able to bear against the great Aufidius
80 A shield as hard as his. A certain number,
Though thanks to all, must I select from all. The rest
Shall bear the business in some other fight,
As cause will be obeyed. Please you to march;
And I shall quickly draw out my command,
Which men are best inclined.

COMINIUS                    March on, my fellows.
Make good this ostentation, and you shall
Divide in all with us.                    *Exeunt*


I.7      *Titus Lartius, having set a guard upon Corioles,
         going with Drum and Trumpet toward Cominius and
         Caius Martius, enters with a Lieutenant, other Sol-
         diers, and a Scout*

LARTIUS
So, let the ports be guarded. Keep your duties
As I have set them down. If I do send, dispatch
Those centuries to our aid. The rest will serve
For a short holding. If we lose the field,
We cannot keep the town.

LIEUTENANT                    Fear not our care, sir.
LARTIUS
Hence, and shut your gates upon's.
Our guider, come; to th'Roman camp conduct us.
                                      *Exeunt*

*Alarum, as in battle. Enter Martius and Aufidius at*   I.8
*several doors*

MARTIUS
  I'll fight with none but thee, for I do hate thee
  Worse than a promise-breaker.

AUFIDIUS                              We hate alike.
  Not Afric owns a serpent I abhor
  More than thy fame and envy. Fix thy foot.

MARTIUS
  Let the first budger die the other's slave,
  And the gods doom him after.

AUFIDIUS                              If I fly, Martius,
  Holloa me like a hare.

MARTIUS                    Within these three hours, Tullus,
  Alone I fought in your Corioles walls,
  And made what work I pleased. 'Tis not my blood
  Wherein thou seest me masked. For thy revenge                 10
  Wrench up thy power to th'highest.

AUFIDIUS                              Wert thou the Hector
  That was the whip of your bragged progeny,
  Thou shouldst not scape me here.

        *Here they fight, and certain Volsces come in the aid of*
        *Aufidius. Martius fights till they be driven in breath-*
        *less*
  Officious and not valiant, you have shamed me
  In your condemnèd seconds.                    *Exeunt*


        *Flourish. Alarum. A retreat is sounded. Enter, at one*   I.9
        *door, Cominius, with the Romans; at another door,*
        *Martius, with his arm in a scarf*

COMINIUS
  If I should tell thee o'er this thy day's work,
  Thou't not believe thy deeds. But I'll report it

83

Where senators shall mingle tears with smiles;
Where great patricians shall attend and shrug,
I'th'end admire; where ladies shall be frighted
And, gladly quaked, hear more; where the dull tribunes,
That with the fusty plebeians hate thine honours,
Shall say against their hearts 'We thank the gods
Our Rome hath such a soldier.'

10    Yet cam'st thou to a morsel of this feast,
Having fully dined before.

       *Enter Titus Lartius, with his power, from the pursuit*

LARTIUS              O general,
Here is the steed, we the caparison.
Hadst thou beheld –

MARTIUS           Pray now, no more. My mother,
Who has a charter to extol her blood,
When she does praise me grieves me. I have done
As you have done – that's what I can; induced
As you have been – that's for my country.
He that has but effected his good will
Hath overta'en mine act.

COMINIUS             You shall not be
20    The grave of your deserving. Rome must know
The value of her own. 'Twere a concealment
Worse than a theft, no less than a traducement,
To hide your doings and to silence that
Which, to the spire and top of praises vouched,
Would seem but modest. Therefore, I beseech you –
In sign of what you are, not to reward
What you have done – before our army hear me.

MARTIUS
I have some wounds upon me, and they smart
To hear themselves remembered.

COMINIUS            Should they not,
30    Well might they fester 'gainst ingratitude

84

And tent themselves with death. Of all the horses –
Whereof we have ta'en good and good store – of all
The treasure in this field achieved and city,
We render you the tenth, to be ta'en forth
Before the common distribution at
Your only choice.

MARTIUS            I thank you, general,
But cannot make my heart consent to take
A bribe to pay my sword. I do refuse it,
And stand upon my common part with those
That have beheld the doing.                              40

> *A long flourish. They all cry 'Martius! Martius!',*
> *cast up their caps and lances. Cominius and Lartius*
> *stand bare*

MARTIUS

May these same instruments which you profane
Never sound more! When drums and trumpets shall
I'th'field prove flatterers, let courts and cities be
Made all of false-faced soothing. When steel grows
Soft as the parasite's silk, let him be made
An overture for th'wars. No more, I say.
For that I have not washed my nose that bled,
Or foiled some debile wretch, which without note
Here's many else have done, you shout me forth
In acclamations hyperbolical,                            50
As if I loved my little should be dieted
In praises sauced with lies.

COMINIUS                      Too modest are you,
More cruel to your good report than grateful
To us that give you truly. By your patience,
If 'gainst yourself you be incensed, we'll put you –
Like one that means his proper harm – in manacles,
Then reason safely with you. Therefore be it known,
As to us, to all the world, that Caius Martius

Wears this war's garland; in token of the which,

60 My noble steed, known to the camp, I give him,
With all his trim belonging; and from this time,
For what he did before Corioles, call him
With all th'applause and clamour of the host,
Caius Martius Coriolanus.
Bear th'addition nobly ever!

*Flourish. Trumpets sound, and drums*

ALL
Caius Martius Coriolanus!

CORIOLANUS
I will go wash;
And when my face is fair you shall perceive
Whether I blush or no. Howbeit, I thank you.

70 I mean to stride your steed, and at all times
To undercrest your good addition
To th'fairness of my power.

COMINIUS                    So, to our tent,
Where, ere we do repose us, we will write
To Rome of our success. You, Titus Lartius,
Must to Corioles back. Send us to Rome
The best, with whom we may articulate
For their own good and ours.

LARTIUS                    I shall, my lord.

CORIOLANUS
The gods begin to mock me. I, that now
Refused most princely gifts, am bound to beg

80 Of my lord general.

COMINIUS                    Take't, 'tis yours. What is't?

CORIOLANUS
I sometime lay here in Corioles
At a poor man's house; he used me kindly.
He cried to me; I saw him prisoner;
But then Aufidius was within my view,

86

And wrath o'erwhelmed my pity. I request you
To give my poor host freedom.

COMINIUS                             O, well begged!
Were he the butcher of my son, he should
Be free as is the wind. Deliver him, Titus.

LARTIUS
Martius, his name?

CORIOLANUS          By Jupiter, forgot!
I am weary; yea, my memory is tired.                    90
Have we no wine here?

COMINIUS                             Go we to our tent.
The blood upon your visage dries, 'tis time
It should be looked to. Come.          *Exeunt*

*dénovement
(the way
things
turn out*


*A flourish. Cornets. Enter Tullus Aufidius, bloody,*   I.10
*with two or three Soldiers*

AUFIDIUS
The town is ta'en.

FIRST SOLDIER          *favourable terms*
'Twill be delivered back on good condition.

AUFIDIUS
Condition?
I would I were a Roman, for I cannot,
Being a Volsce, be that I am. Condition?
What good condition can a treaty find
I'th'part that is at mercy? Five times, Martius,
I have fought with thee; so often hast thou beat me;
And wouldst do so, I think, should we encounter
As often as we eat. By th'elements,                    10
If e'er again I meet him beard to beard,
He's mine or I am his. Mine emulation
Hath not that honour in't it had; for where
I thought to crush him in an equal force,

87

    True sword to sword, I'll potch at him some way
    Or wrath or craft may get him.

FIRST SOLDIER              He's the devil.

AUFIDIUS
    Bolder, though not so subtle. My valour's poisoned
    With only suffering stain by him; for him
    Shall fly out of itself. Nor sleep nor sanctuary,
20  Being naked, sick, nor fane nor Capitol,
    The prayers of priests nor times of sacrifice,
    Embarquements all of fury, shall lift up
    Their rotten privilege and custom 'gainst
    My hate to Martius. Where I find him, were it
    At home upon my brother's guard, even there,
    Against the hospitable canon, would I
    Wash my fierce hand in's heart. Go you to th'city.
    Learn how 'tis held, and what they are that must
    Be hostages for Rome.

FIRST SOLDIER        Will not you go?

AUFIDIUS
30  I am attended at the cypress grove. I pray you –
    'Tis south the city mills – bring me word thither
    How the world goes, that to the pace of it
    I may spur on my journey.

FIRST SOLDIER       I shall, sir.      *Exeunt*

\*

II.1     *Enter Menenius, with the two Tribunes of the People,*
       *Sicinius and Brutus*

MENENIUS The augurer tells me we shall have news to-
    night.

BRUTUS Good or bad?

MENENIUS Not according to the prayer of the people, for they love not Martius.

SICINIUS Nature teaches beasts to know their friends.

MENENIUS Pray you, who does the wolf love?

SICINIUS The lamb.

MENENIUS Ay, to devour him, as the hungry plebeians would the noble Martius.                                        10

BRUTUS He's a lamb indeed, that baas like a bear.

MENENIUS He's a bear indeed, that lives like a lamb. You two are old men; tell me one thing that I shall ask you.

BOTH Well, sir?

MENENIUS In what enormity is Martius poor in that you two have not in abundance?

BRUTUS He's poor in no one fault, but stored with all.

SICINIUS Especially in pride.

BRUTUS And topping all others in boasting.

MENENIUS This is strange now. Do you two know how  20 you are censured here in the city – I mean of us o'th' right-hand file? Do you?

BOTH Why, how are we censured?

MENENIUS Because you talk of pride now – will you not be angry?

BOTH Well, well, sir, well?

MENENIUS Why, 'tis no great matter, for a very little thief of occasion will rob you of a great deal of patience. Give your dispositions the reins and be angry at your pleasures – at the least, if you take it as a pleasure to you  30 in being so. You blame Martius for being proud?

BRUTUS We do it not alone, sir.

MENENIUS I know you can do very little alone, for your helps are many, or else your actions would grow wondrous single. Your abilities are too infant-like for doing much alone. You talk of pride. O that you could turn your eyes toward the napes of your necks, and make but an interior survey of your good selves! O that you could!

BOTH What then, sir?

40 MENENIUS Why, then you should discover a brace of un-
meriting, proud, violent, testy magistrates – alias fools –
as any in Rome.

SICINIUS Menenius, you are known well enough too.

MENENIUS I am known to be a humorous patrician, and
one that loves a cup of hot wine with not a drop of allay-
ing Tiber in't; said to be something imperfect in favouring the first complaint, hasty and tinder-like upon too
trivial motion; one that converses more with the buttock of the night than with the forehead of the morning.

50 What I think I utter, and spend my malice in my breath.
Meeting two such wealsmen as you are – I cannot call
you Lycurguses – if the drink you give me touch my
palate adversely, I make a crooked face at it. I cannot
say your worships have delivered the matter well, when
I find the ass in compound with the major part of your
syllables. And though I must be content to bear with
those that say you are reverend grave men, yet they lie
deadly that tell you have good faces. If you see this in the
map of my microcosm, follows it that I am known well

60 enough too? What harm can your bisson conspectuities
glean out of this character, if I be known well enough too?

BRUTUS Come, sir, come, we know you well enough.

MENENIUS You know neither me, yourselves, nor any
thing. You are ambitious for poor knaves' caps and legs.
You wear out a good wholesome forenoon in hearing a
cause between an orange-wife and a faucet-seller, and
then rejourn the controversy of threepence to a second
day of audience. When you are hearing a matter between
party and party, if you chance to be pinched with the

70 colic, you make faces like mummers, set up the bloody
flag against all patience, and, in roaring for a chamber-

pot, dismiss the controversy bleeding, the more entangled by your hearing. All the peace you make in their
cause is calling both the parties knaves. You are a pair of
strange ones.

BRUTUS Come, come, you are well understood to be a perfecter giber for the table than a necessary bencher in the
Capitol.

MENENIUS Our very priests must become mockers, if they
shall encounter such ridiculous subjects as you are. 80
When you speak best unto the purpose, it is not worth
the wagging of your beards; and your beards deserve not
so honourable a grave as to stuff a botcher's cushion or to
be entombed in an ass's pack-saddle. Yet you must be
saying Martius is proud; who, in a cheap estimation, is
worth all your predecessors since Deucalion, though
peradventure some of the best of 'em were hereditary
hangmen. Good-e'en to your worships. More of your
conversation would infect my brain, being the herdsmen
of the beastly plebeians. I will be bold to take my leave 90
of you.

*Brutus and Sicinius stand aside*
*Enter Volumnia, Virgilia, and Valeria*

How now, my as fair as noble ladies – and the moon,
were she earthly, no nobler – whither do you follow your
eyes so fast?

VOLUMNIA Honourable Menenius, my boy Martius
approaches. For the love of Juno, let's go.

MENENIUS Ha? Martius coming home?

VOLUMNIA Ay, worthy Menenius, and with most prosperous approbation.

MENENIUS Take my cap, Jupiter, and I thank thee. Hoo! 100
Martius coming home?

VIRGILIA *and* VALERIA Nay, 'tis true.

VOLUMNIA Look, here's a letter from him. The state hath

another, his wife another, and I think there's one at home for you.

MENENIUS I will make my very house reel tonight. A letter for me?

VIRGILIA Yes, certain, there's a letter for you, I saw't.

MENENIUS A letter for me! It gives me an estate of seven
110    years' health, in which time I will make a lip at the physician. The most sovereign prescription in Galen is but empiricutic and, to this preservative, of no better report than a horse-drench. Is he not wounded? He was wont to come home wounded.

VIRGILIA O, no, no, no.

VOLUMNIA O, he is wounded, I thank the gods for't.

MENENIUS So do I too – if it be not too much. Brings 'a victory in his pocket, the wounds become him.

VOLUMNIA On's brows, Menenius. He comes the third
120    time home with the oaken garland.

MENENIUS Has he disciplined Aufidius soundly?

VOLUMNIA Titus Lartius writes they fought together, but Aufidius got off.

MENENIUS And 'twas time for him too, I'll warrant him that. An he had stayed by him, I would not have been so fidiused for all the chests in Corioles and the gold that's in them. Is the Senate possessed of this?

VOLUMNIA Good ladies, let's go. Yes, yes, yes! The Senate has letters from the general, wherein he gives
130    my son the whole name of the war. He hath in this action outdone his former deeds doubly.

VALERIA In troth, there's wondrous things spoke of him.

MENENIUS Wondrous? Ay, I warrant you, and not without his true purchasing.

VIRGILIA The gods grant them true.

VOLUMNIA True? Pow waw!

MENENIUS True? I'll be sworn they are true. Where is

he wounded? (*To the Tribunes*) God save your good worships! Martius is coming home. He has more cause to be proud. – Where is he wounded?

VOLUMNIA I'th'shoulder and i'th'left arm. There will be large cicatrices to show the people, when he shall stand for his place. He received in the repulse of Tarquin seven hurts i'th'body.

MENENIUS One i'th'neck and two i'th'thigh – there's nine that I know.

VOLUMNIA He had before this last expedition twenty-five wounds upon him.

MENENIUS Now it's twenty-seven. Every gash was an enemy's grave. (*A shout and flourish*) Hark, the trumpets.

VOLUMNIA These are the ushers of Martius. Before him he carries noise, and behind him he leaves tears.
Death, that dark spirit, in's nervy arm doth lie,
Which, being advanced, declines, and then men die.

> *A sennet. Trumpets sound. Enter Cominius the General and Titus Lartius; between them, Coriolanus, crowned with an oaken garland; with Captains and Soldiers and a Herald*

HERALD

Know, Rome, that all alone Martius did fight
Within Corioles gates, where he hath won,
With fame, a name to Caius Martius; these
In honour follows 'Coriolanus'.
Welcome to Rome, renownèd Coriolanus!

> *Sound flourish*

ALL

Welcome to Rome, renownèd Coriolanus!

CORIOLANUS

No more of this; it does offend my heart.
Pray now, no more.

COMINIUS                 Look, sir, your mother!

CORIOLANUS                                             O,
You have, I know, petitioned all the gods
For my prosperity!
       *He kneels*

VOLUMNIA           Nay, my good soldier, up,
My gentle Martius, worthy Caius, and
By deed-achieving honour newly named –
What is it? – Coriolanus must I call thee? –
But, O, thy wife!

CORIOLANUS       My gracious silence, hail!
Wouldst thou have laughed had I come coffined home,
170   That weep'st to see me triumph? Ah, my dear,
Such eyes the widows in Corioles wear,
And mothers that lack sons.

MENENIUS                     Now the gods crown thee!

CORIOLANUS
And live you yet? (*To Valeria*) O my sweet lady, pardon.

VOLUMNIA
I know not where to turn. O, welcome home.
And welcome, general, and y'are welcome all.

MENENIUS
A hundred thousand welcomes. I could weep
And I could laugh, I am light and heavy. Welcome.
A curse begin at very root on's heart
That is not glad to see thee. You are three
180   That Rome should dote on. Yet, by the faith of men,
We have some old crab-trees here at home that will not
Be grafted to your relish. Yet welcome, warriors.
We call a nettle but a nettle and
The faults of fools but folly.

COMINIUS                 Ever right.

CORIOLANUS
Menenius, ever, ever.

94

HERALD

Give way there, and go on.

CORIOLANUS (*to Volumnia and Virgilia*)

                              Your hand, and yours.
Ere in our own house I do shade my head,
The good patricians must be visited,
From whom I have received not only greetings,
But with them change of honours.

VOLUMNIA                              I have lived                    190
To see inherited my very wishes
And the buildings of my fancy. Only
There's one thing wanting, which I doubt not but
Our Rome will cast upon thee.

CORIOLANUS                    Know, good mother,
I had rather be their servant in my way
Than sway with them in theirs.

COMINIUS                          On, to the Capitol.

          *Flourish. Cornets. Exeunt in state, as before.*
          *Brutus and Sicinius come forward*

BRUTUS

All tongues speak of him and the blearèd sights
Are spectacled to see him. Your prattling nurse
Into a rapture lets her baby cry
While she chats him. The kitchen malkin pins          200
Her richest lockram 'bout her reechy neck,
Clambering the walls to eye him. Stalls, bulks, windows
Are smothered up, leads filled, and ridges horsed
With variable complexions, all agreeing
In earnestness to see him. Seld-shown flamens
Do press among the popular throngs and puff
To win a vulgar station. Our veiled dames
Commit the war of white and damask in
Their nicely gawded cheeks to th'wanton spoil
Of Phoebus' burning kisses. Such a pother          210

95

As if that whatsoever god who leads him
Were slily crept into his human powers
And gave him graceful posture.

SICINIUS                               On the sudden
I warrant him consul.

BRUTUS                    Then our office may
During his power go sleep.

SICINIUS
He cannot temperately transport his honours
From where he should begin and end, but will
Lose those he hath won.

BRUTUS                    In that there's comfort.

SICINIUS                                              Doubt not
The commoners, for whom we stand, but they
220    Upon their ancient malice will forget
With the least cause these his new honours, which
That he will give them make I as little question
As he is proud to do't.

BRUTUS                    I heard him swear,
Were he to stand for consul, never would he
Appear i'th'market-place nor on him put
The napless vesture of humility,
Nor showing, as the manner is, his wounds
To th'people, beg their stinking breaths.

SICINIUS                                              'Tis right.

BRUTUS
It was his word. O, he would miss it rather
230    Than carry it but by the suit of the gentry to him
And the desire of the nobles.

SICINIUS                    I wish no better
Than have him hold that purpose and to put it
In execution.

BRUTUS          'Tis most like he will.

SICINIUS

It shall be to him then as our good wills, *prophecy of the downfall to come*
A sure destruction.

BRUTUS                    So it must fall out
To him, or our authority's for an end.
We must suggest the people in what hatred
He still hath held them; that to's power he would
Have made them mules, silenced their pleaders and
Dispropertied their freedoms, holding them                    240
In human action and capacity
Of no more soul nor fitness for the world
Than camels in the war, who have their provand *food*
Only for bearing burdens, and sore blows
For sinking under them.

SICINIUS                    This, as you say, suggested
At some time when his soaring insolence
Shall teach the people – which time shall not want,
If he be put upon't, and that's as easy
As to set dogs on sheep – will be his fire
To kindle their dry stubble; and their blaze                    250
Shall darken him for ever.

*Enter a Messenger*

BRUTUS                    What's the matter?

MESSENGER

You are sent for to the Capitol. 'Tis thought
That Martius shall be consul.
I have seen the dumb men throng to see him and
The blind to hear him speak. Matrons flung gloves,
Ladies and maids their scarfs and handkerchers,
Upon him as he passed. The nobles bended
As to Jove's statue, and the commons made
A shower and thunder with their caps and shouts.
I never saw the like.

BRUTUS                    Let's to the Capitol,                    260

97

And carry with us ears and eyes for th'time,
But hearts for the event.

SICINIUS                    Have with you.          *Exeunt*


II.2          *Enter two Officers, to lay cushions, as it were in the*
             *Capitol*

FIRST OFFICER Come, come, they are almost here. How
many stand for consulships?

SECOND OFFICER Three, they say; but 'tis thought of
everyone Coriolanus will carry it.

FIRST OFFICER That's a brave fellow, but he's vengeance
proud and loves not the common people.

SECOND OFFICER Faith, there hath been many great men
that have flattered the people, who ne'er loved them; and
there be many that they have loved, they know not
10  wherefore. So that, if they love they know not why, they
hate upon no better a ground. Therefore, for Coriolanus
neither to care whether they love or hate him manifests
the true knowledge he has in their disposition, and out of
his noble carelessness lets them plainly see't.

FIRST OFFICER If he did not care whether he had their
love or no, he waved indifferently 'twixt doing them
neither good nor harm. But he seeks their hate with
greater devotion than they can render it him, and leaves
nothing undone that may fully discover him their oppo-
20  site. Now to seem to affect the malice and displeasure of
the people is as bad as that which he dislikes – to flatter
them for their love.

SECOND OFFICER He hath deserved worthily of his country; and his ascent is not by such easy degrees as those
who, having been supple and courteous to the people,
bonneted, without any further deed to have them at all,
into their estimation and report. But he hath so planted

98

his honours in their eyes and his actions in their hearts
that for their tongues to be silent and not confess so much
were a kind of ingrateful injury. To report otherwise  30
were a malice that, giving itself the lie, would pluck
reproof and rebuke from every ear that heard it.

FIRST OFFICER No more of him, he's a worthy man.
Make way, they are coming.

*A sennet. Enter the Patricians and the Tribunes of the
People, Lictors before them; Coriolanus, Menenius,
Cominius the Consul. Sicinius and Brutus take their
places by themselves*

MENENIUS
Having determined of the Volsces and
To send for Titus Lartius, it remains,
As the main point of this our after-meeting,
To gratify his noble service that
Hath thus stood for his country. Therefore please you,
Most reverend and grave elders, to desire  40
The present consul and last general
In our well-found successes to report
A little of that worthy work performed
By Caius Martius Coriolanus, whom
We met here both to thank and to remember
With honours like himself.

FIRST SENATOR                Speak, good Cominius.
Leave nothing out for length, and make us think
Rather our state's defective for requital
Than we to stretch it out. (*To the Tribunes*) Masters
        o'th'people,
We do request your kindest ears, and after,  50
Your loving motion toward the common body
To yield what passes here.

SICINIUS                We are convented
Upon a pleasing treaty, and have hearts

99

Inclinable to honour and advance
The theme of our assembly.

BRUTUS                              Which the rather
We shall be blessed to do, if he remember
A kinder value of the people than
He hath hereto prized them at.

MENENIUS                          That's off, that's off!
I would you rather had been silent. Please you
60   To hear Cominius speak?

BRUTUS                          Most willingly.
But yet my caution was more pertinent
Than the rebuke you give it.

MENENIUS                          He loves your people;
But tie him not to be their bedfellow.
Worthy Cominius, speak.

> *Coriolanus rises, and offers to go away*
                              Nay, keep your place.

FIRST SENATOR
Sit, Coriolanus, never shame to hear
What you have nobly done.

CORIOLANUS                      Your honours' pardon.
I had rather have my wounds to heal again
Than hear say how I got them.

BRUTUS                          Sir, I hope
My words disbenched you not.

CORIOLANUS                      No, sir. Yet oft,
70   When blows have made me stay, I fled from words.
You soothed not, therefore hurt not. But your people,
I love them as they weigh –

MENENIUS                      Pray now, sit down.

CORIOLANUS
I had rather have one scratch my head i'th'sun
When the alarum were struck than idly sit
To hear my nothings monstered.        *Exit Coriolanus*

MENENIUS                          Masters of the people,
Your multiplying spawn how can he flatter –
That's thousand to one good one – when you now see
He had rather venture all his limbs for honour
Than one on's ears to hear it. Proceed, Cominius.

COMINIUS
I shall lack voice. The deeds of Coriolanus                    80
Should not be uttered feebly. It is held
That valour is the chiefest virtue and
Most dignifies the haver. If it be,        *Cominius is not*
                                           *convinced it is*
The man I speak of cannot in the world           *so*
Be singly counterpoised. At sixteen years,
                                           *raised an army*
When Tarquin made a head for Rome, he fought   *power*
Beyond the mark of others. Our then dictator,
Whom with all praise I point at, saw him fight
                              *beardless*
When with his Amazonian chin he drove   *eldermen*
The bristled lips before him. He bestrid             90
An o'erpressed Roman and i'th'Consul's view
*his*   Slew three opposers. Tarquin's self he met,
*nose*  And struck him on his knee. In that day's feats,
When he might act the woman in the scene,  *When he was still*
He proved best man i'th'field, and for his meed  *a' boy*
                                         *reward*
Was brow-bound with the oak. His pupil age
Man-entered thus, he waxèd like a sea,
And in the brunt of seventeen battles since
*one*   He lurched all swords of the garland. For this last,
*ined*  Before and in Corioles, let me say               100
*e*                           *do him justice*
*ttle*  I cannot speak him home. He stopped the fliers,
*nours* And by his rare example made the coward
Turn terror into sport. As weeds before
A vessel under sail, so men obeyed      *metaphor*
And fell below his stem. His sword, death's stamp,  *metaphor*
                        *killed*
Where it did mark, it took from face to foot.
He was a thing of blood, whose every motion

## II.2

Was timed with dying cries. Alone he entered
The mortal gate of th'city, which he painted with blood
110   With shunless destiny; aidless came off,
And with a sudden reinforcement struck              metaphor
Corioles like a planet. Now all's his,              the other
When by and by the din of war 'gan pierce           war
His ready sense, then straight his doubled spirit
Requickened what in flesh was fatigate,
And to the battle came he, where he did
Run reeking o'er the lives of men, as if
'Twere a perpetual spoil; and till we called
Both field and city ours he never stood
120   To ease his breast with panting.

MENENIUS                              Worthy man!

FIRST SENATOR

He cannot but with measure fit the honours
Which we devise him.

COMINIUS                Our spoils he kicked at,
And looked upon things precious as they were
The common muck of the world. He covets less
Than misery itself would give, rewards
His deeds with doing them, and is content
To spend the time to end it.

MENENIUS                              He's right noble.
Let him be called for.

FIRST SENATOR          Call Coriolanus.

*Enter Coriolanus*

OFFICER

He doth appear.

MENENIUS

130   The Senate, Coriolanus, are well pleased
To make thee consul.

CORIOLANUS            I do owe them still
My life and services.

102

MENENIUS                It then remains
  That you do speak to the people.

CORIOLANUS                          I do beseech you
  Let me o'erleap that custom, for I cannot
  Put on the gown, stand naked, and entreat them
  For my wounds' sake to give their suffrage. Please you
  That I may pass this doing.

SICINIUS                      Sir, the people
  Must have their voices, neither will they bate
  One jot of ceremony.

MENENIUS                Put them not to't.
  Pray you go fit you to the custom and                    140
  Take to you, as your predecessors have,
  Your honour with your form.

CORIOLANUS                    It is a part
  That I shall blush in acting, and might well
  Be taken from the people.

BRUTUS (*to Sicinius*)       Mark you that?

CORIOLANUS
  To brag unto them 'Thus I did, and thus!',
  Show them th'unaching scars which I should hide,
  As if I had received them for the hire
  Of their breath only!

MENENIUS               Do not stand upon't.
  We recommend to you, Tribunes of the People,
  Our purpose to them; and to our noble Consul         150
  Wish we all joy and honour.

SENATORS
  To Coriolanus come all joy and honour!
                    *Flourish. Cornets. Then exeunt.*
      *Sicinius and Brutus stay behind*

BRUTUS
  You see how he intends to use the people.

103

SICINIUS

May they perceive's intent! He will require them
As if he did contemn what he requested
Should be in them to give.

BRUTUS                              Come, we'll inform them
Of our proceedings here. On th'market-place
I know they do attend us.                              *Exeunt*

II.3          *Enter seven or eight Citizens*

FIRST CITIZEN Once, if he do require our voices, we
ought not to deny him.

SECOND CITIZEN We may, sir, if we will.

THIRD CITIZEN We have power in ourselves to do it, but
it is a power that we have no power to do. For if he show
us his wounds and tell us his deeds, we are to put our
tongues into those wounds and speak for them. So, if he
tell us his noble deeds, we must also tell him our noble
acceptance of them. Ingratitude is monstrous, and for
10  the multitude to be ingrateful were to make a monster of
the multitude; of the which we being members should
bring ourselves to be monstrous members.

FIRST CITIZEN And to make us no better thought of a
little help will serve; for once we stood up about the
corn, he himself stuck not to call us the many-headed
multitude.

THIRD CITIZEN We have been called so of many; not
that our heads are some brown, some black, some abram,
some bald, but that our wits are so diversely coloured.
20  And truly I think if all our wits were to issue out of one
skull, they would fly east, west, north, south, and their
consent of one direct way should be at once to all the
points o'th'compass.

SECOND CITIZEN Think you so? Which way do you judge my wit would fly?

THIRD CITIZEN Nay, your wit will not so soon out as another man's will – 'tis strongly wedged up in a block-head; but if it were at liberty 'twould sure southward.

SECOND CITIZEN Why that way?

THIRD CITIZEN To lose itself in a fog, where being three parts melted away with rotten dews, the fourth would return for conscience' sake to help to get thee a wife. 30

SECOND CITIZEN You are never without your tricks. You may, you may!

THIRD CITIZEN Are you all resolved to give your voices? But that's no matter, the greater part carries it. I say, if he would incline to the people, there was never a worthier man.

> *Enter Coriolanus in a gown of humility, with Menenius*

Here he comes, and in the gown of humility. Mark his behaviour. We are not to stay all together, but to come by him where he stands, by ones, by twos, and by threes. He's to make his requests by particulars, wherein every one of us has a single honour, in giving him our own voices with our own tongues. Therefore follow me, and I'll direct you how you shall go by him. 40

ALL Content, content. *Exeunt Citizens*

MENENIUS

O sir, you are not right. Have you not known
The worthiest men have done't?

CORIOLANUS                    What must I say? –
'I pray, sir' – Plague upon't! I cannot bring
My tongue to such a pace. 'Look, sir, my wounds! 50
I got them in my country's service, when
Some certain of your brethren roared and ran
From th'noise of our own drums.'

MENENIUS                              O me, the gods!
You must not speak of that. You must desire them
To think upon you.

CORIOLANUS              Think upon me? Hang 'em!
I would they would forget me, like the virtues
Which our divines lose by 'em.

MENENIUS                      You'll mar all.
I'll leave you. Pray you speak to 'em, I pray you,
In wholesome manner.                              *Exit*

          *Enter three of the Citizens*

CORIOLANUS              Bid them wash their faces
60  And keep their teeth clean. So, here comes a brace.
You know the cause, sir, of my standing here.

THIRD CITIZEN
We do, sir. Tell us what hath brought you to't.

CORIOLANUS Mine own desert.

SECOND CITIZEN Your own desert?

CORIOLANUS Ay, but not mine own desire.

THIRD CITIZEN How not your own desire?

CORIOLANUS No, sir, 'twas never my desire yet to trouble
the poor with begging.

THIRD CITIZEN You must think, if we give you anything,
70  we hope to gain by you.

CORIOLANUS Well then, I pray, your price o'th'consulship?

FIRST CITIZEN The price is to ask it kindly.

CORIOLANUS Kindly, sir, I pray let me ha't. I have
wounds to show you, which shall be yours in private.
(*to the Second Citizen*) Your good voice, sir. What say
you?

SECOND CITIZEN You shall ha't, worthy sir.

CORIOLANUS A match, sir. There's in all two worthy
80  voices begged. I have your alms. Adieu.

THIRD CITIZEN But this is something odd.

SECOND CITIZEN An 'twere to give again – but 'tis no
matter. *Exeunt*

    *Enter two other Citizens*

CORIOLANUS Pray you now, if it may stand with the tune
of your voices that I may be consul, I have here the customary gown.

FOURTH CITIZEN You have deserved nobly of your
country, and you have not deserved nobly.

CORIOLANUS Your enigma?

FOURTH CITIZEN You have been a scourge to her 90
enemies, you have been a rod to her friends. You have
not indeed loved the common people.

CORIOLANUS You should account me the more virtuous
that I have not been common in my love. I will, sir, flatter my sworn brother, the people, to earn a dearer estimation of them. 'Tis a condition they account gentle;
and since the wisdom of their choice is rather to have my
hat than my heart, I will practise the insinuating nod and
be off to them most counterfeitly. That is, sir, I will
counterfeit the bewitchment of some popular man and 100
give it bountiful to the desirers. Therefore, beseech you
I may be consul.

FIFTH CITIZEN We hope to find you our friend, and
therefore give you our voices heartily.

FOURTH CITIZEN You have received many wounds for
your country.

CORIOLANUS I will not seal your knowledge with showing
them. I will make much of your voices and so trouble
you no farther.

BOTH The gods give you joy, sir, heartily! *Exeunt* 110

CORIOLANUS
  Most sweet voices!
  Better it is to die, better to starve,
  Than crave the hire which first we do deserve.
  Why in this wolvish toge should I stand here

To beg of Hob and Dick that does appear
Their needless vouches? Custom calls me to't.
What custom wills, in all things should we do't,
The dust on antique time would lie unswept
And mountainous error be too highly heaped
120 For truth to o'erpeer. Rather than fool it so,
Let the high office and the honour go
To one that would do thus. I am half through;
The one part suffered, the other will I do.
          *Enter three Citizens more*
Here come more voices.
Your voices! For your voices I have fought,
Watched for your voices; for your voices bear
Of wounds two dozen odd. Battles thrice six
I have seen and heard of; for your voices have
Done many things, some less, some more. Your voices!
130 Indeed, I would be consul.

SIXTH CITIZEN He has done nobly, and cannot go without any honest man's voice.

SEVENTH CITIZEN Therefore let him be consul. The
gods give him joy and make him good friend to the
people!

ALL
Amen, amen. God save thee, noble Consul!
                                        *Exeunt Citizens*

CORIOLANUS Worthy voices.
          *Enter Menenius, with Brutus and Sicinius*
MENENIUS
You have stood your limitation, and the Tribunes
Endue you with the people's voice. Remains
140 That in th'official marks invested you
Anon do meet the Senate.

CORIOLANUS                    Is this done?

SICINIUS
The custom of request you have discharged.

The people do admit you, and are summoned
To meet anon upon your approbation.

*[handwritten: caption the appointment]*

CORIOLANUS

Where? At the Senate House?

SICINIUS                              There, Coriolanus.

CORIOLANUS

May I change these garments?

SICINIUS                              You may, sir.

CORIOLANUS

That I'll straight do and, knowing myself again,
Repair to th'Senate House.

MENENIUS

I'll keep you company. (*To the Tribunes*) Will you along?

BRUTUS

We stay here for the people.

SICINIUS                              Fare you well.                 150

*Exeunt Coriolanus and Menenius*

He has it now, and by his looks methinks
'Tis warm at's heart.

BRUTUS                              With a proud heart he wore
His humble weeds. Will you dismiss the people?

*Enter the Plebeians*

SICINIUS

How now, my masters, have you chose this man?

FIRST CITIZEN

He has our voices, sir.

BRUTUS

We pray the gods he may deserve your loves.

SECOND CITIZEN

Amen, sir. To my poor unworthy notice,
He mocked us when he begged our voices.

THIRD CITIZEN                              Certainly,
He flouted us downright.

FIRST CITIZEN

No, 'tis his kind of speech *[handwritten: way of speaking]* – he did not mock us.          160

SECOND CITIZEN

   Not one amongst us, save yourself, but says
   He used us scornfully. He should have showed us
   His marks of merit, wounds received for's country.

SICINIUS

   Why, so he did, I am sure.

ALL                        No, no! No man saw 'em.

THIRD CITIZEN

   He said he had wounds which he could show in private,
   And with his hat, thus waving it in scorn,
   'I would be consul,' says he. 'Aged custom
   But by your voices will not so permit me;
   Your voices therefore.' When we granted that,
170   Here was 'I thank you for your voices. Thank you,
   Your most sweet voices. Now you have left your voices,
   I have no further with you.' Was not this mockery?

SICINIUS

   Why either were you ignorant to see't,
   Or, seeing it, of such childish friendliness
   To yield your voices?

BRUTUS             Could you not have told him –
   As you were lessoned – when he had no power,
   But was a petty servant to the state,
   He was your enemy, ever spake against
   Your liberties and the charters that you bear
180   I'th'body of the weal; and now, arriving
   A place of potency and sway o'th'state,
   If he should still malignantly remain
   Fast foe to th'plebeii, your voices might
   Be curses to yourselves? You should have said
   That as his worthy deeds did claim no less
   Than what he stood for, so his gracious nature
   Would think upon you for your voices and
   Translate his malice towards you into love,

Standing your friendly lord.

SICINIUS                  Thus to have said,
As you were fore-advised, had touched his spirit      190
And tried his inclination; from him plucked
Either his gracious promise, which you might,
As cause had called you up, have held him to;
Or else it would have galled his surly nature,
Which easily endures not article
Tying him to aught. So putting him to rage,
You should have ta'en th'advantage of his choler
And passed him unelected.

BRUTUS                Did you perceive
He did solicit you in free contempt
When he did need your loves, and do you think     200
That his contempt shall not be bruising to you
When he hath power to crush? Why, had your bodies
No heart among you? Or had you tongues to cry
Against the rectorship of judgement?

SICINIUS                  Have you
Ere now denied the asker, and now again,
Of him that did not ask but mock, bestow
Your sued-for tongues?

THIRD CITIZEN
He's not confirmed; we may deny him yet.

SECOND CITIZEN
And will deny him.
I'll have five hundred voices of that sound.     210

FIRST CITIZEN
I twice five hundred, and their friends to piece 'em.

BRUTUS
Get you hence instantly, and tell those friends
They have chose a consul that will from them take
Their liberties, make them of no more voice
Than dogs that are as often beat for barking

As therefore kept to do so.

SICINIUS                    Let them assemble,
And on a safer judgement all revoke
Your ignorant election. Enforce his pride
And his old hate unto you. Besides, forget not
220   With what contempt he wore the humble weed,
How in his suit he scorned you; but your loves,
Thinking upon his services, took from you
Th'apprehension of his present portance,
Which most gibingly, ungravely, he did fashion
After the inveterate hate he bears you.

BRUTUS                                Lay
A fault on us, your Tribunes, that we laboured,
No impediment between, but that you must
Cast your election on him.

SICINIUS                    Say you chose him
More after our commandment than as guided
230   By your own true affections, and that your minds,
Pre-occupied with what you rather must do
Than what you should, made you against the grain
To voice him consul. Lay the fault on us.

BRUTUS
Ay, spare us not. Say we read lectures to you,
How youngly he began to serve his country,
How long continued, and what stock he springs of –
The noble house o'th'Martians, from whence came
That Ancus Martius, Numa's daughter's son,
Who after great Hostilius here was king.
240   Of the same house Publius and Quintus were,
That our best water brought by conduits hither;
And Censorinus, nobly namèd so,
Twice being by the people chosen censor,
Was his great ancestor.

SICINIUS                    One thus descended,

That hath beside well in his person wrought
To be set high in place, we did commend
To your remembrances. But you have found,
Scaling his present bearing with his past,
That he's your fixèd enemy, and revoke
Your sudden approbation.

BRUTUS                    Say you ne'er had done't –    250
Harp on that still – but by our putting on.
And presently, when you have drawn your number,
Repair to th'Capitol.

ALL                    We will so. Almost all
Repent in their election.                    *Exeunt Plebeians*

BRUTUS                    Let them go on.
This mutiny were better put in hazard
Than stay, past doubt, for greater.
If, as his nature is, he fall in rage
With their refusal, both observe and answer
The vantage of his anger.

SICINIUS                    To th'Capitol, come.
We will be there before the stream o'th'people;    260
And this shall seem, as partly 'tis, their own,
Which we have goaded onward.                    *Exeunt*

*Cornets. Enter Coriolanus, Menenius, all the Gentry,*  III.1
     *Cominius, Titus Lartius, and other Senators*

CORIOLANUS
Tullus Aufidius then had made new head?

LARTIUS
He had, my lord, and that it was which caused
Our swifter composition.

113

**III.1**

CORIOLANUS
So then the Volsces stand but as at first,
Ready, when time shall prompt them, to make road
Upon's again.

COMINIUS      They are worn, lord Consul, so
That we shall hardly in our ages see
Their banners wave again.

CORIOLANUS           Saw you Aufidius?

LARTIUS
On safeguard he came to me, and did curse
10   Against the Volsces, for they had so vilely
Yielded the town. He is retired to Antium.

CORIOLANUS
Spoke he of me?

LARTIUS        He did, my lord.

CORIOLANUS          How? What?

LARTIUS
How often he had met you, sword to sword;
That of all things upon the earth he hated
Your person most; that he would pawn his fortunes
To hopeless restitution, so he might
Be called your vanquisher.

CORIOLANUS        At Antium lives he?

LARTIUS
At Antium.

CORIOLANUS
I wish I had a cause to seek him there,
20   To oppose his hatred fully. Welcome home.
     *Enter Sicinius and Brutus*
Behold, these are the Tribunes of the People,
The tongues o'th'common mouth. I do despise them,
For they do prank them in authority
Against all noble sufferance.

114

*stychomythia — short speeches to indicate tension*

SICINIUS                              Pass no further.

CORIOLANUS

Ha? What is that?

BRUTUS

It will be dangerous to go on. No further.

CORIOLANUS

What makes this change?

MENENIUS

The matter?

COMINIUS     *been approved by*

Hath he not (passed) the noble and the common?

BRUTUS

Cominius, no.

CORIOLANUS     Have I had children's voices?     30

FIRST SENATOR

Tribunes, give way. He shall to th'market-place.

BRUTUS

The people are incensed against him.

SICINIUS                              Stop,

Or all will fall in broil.

CORIOLANUS              Are these your herd?

Must these have voices, that can yield them now

And straight disclaim their tongues? What are your
        offices?

You being their mouths, why rule you not their teeth?

Have you not set them on?

MENENIUS              Be calm, be calm.

CORIOLANUS

It is a purposed thing, and grows by plot,

To curb the will of the nobility.

(Suffer't,) and live with such as cannot rule     40

Nor ever will be ruled.

BRUTUS              Call't not a plot.

The people cry you mocked them; and of late,

115

When corn was given them gratis, you repined,
Scandalled the supplants for the people, called them
Time-pleasers, flatterers, foes to nobleness.

CORIOLANUS
Why, this was known before.

BRUTUS                          Not to them all.

CORIOLANUS
Have you informed them sithence?

BRUTUS                          How? I inform them!

COMINIUS
You are like to do such business.

BRUTUS                          Not unlike
Each way to better yours.

CORIOLANUS
50    Why then should I be consul? By yond clouds,
Let me deserve so ill as you, and make me
Your fellow tribune.

SICINIUS                        You show too much of that
For which the people stir. If you will pass
To where you are bound, you must enquire your way,
Which you are out of, with a gentler spirit,
Or never be so noble as a consul,
Nor yoke with him for tribune.

MENENIUS                        Let's be calm.

COMINIUS
The people are abused. Set on. This paltering
Becomes not Rome, nor has Coriolanus
60    Deserved this so dishonoured rub, laid falsely
I'th'plain way of his merit.

CORIOLANUS                      Tell me of corn!
This was my speech, and I will speak't again –

MENENIUS
Not now, not now.

FIRST SENATOR        Not in this heat, sir, now.

CORIOLANUS
Now, as I live I will.
My nobler friends, I crave their pardons. For
The mutable, rank-scented meiny, let them
Regard me as I do not flatter, and
Therein behold themselves. I say again,
In soothing them we nourish 'gainst our Senate
The cockle of rebellion, insolence, sedition,　　　　70
Which we ourselves have ploughed for, sowed, and
　　　　scattered
By mingling them with us, the honoured number,
Who lack not virtue, no, nor power, but that
Which they have given to beggars.

MENENIUS　　　　　　　　Well, no more.

FIRST SENATOR
No more words, we beseech you.

CORIOLANUS　　　　　　　　How? No more?
As for my country I have shed my blood,
Not fearing outward force, so shall my lungs
Coin words till their decay against those measles
Which we disdain should tetter us, yet sought
The very way to catch them.

BRUTUS　　　　　　　　You speak o'th'people　　80
As if you were a god to punish, not
A man of their infirmity.

SICINIUS　　　　　　　　'Twere well
We let the people know't.

MENENIUS　　　　　　　　What, what? His choler?

CORIOLANUS
Choler!
Were I as patient as the midnight sleep,
By Jove, 'twould be my mind.

SICINIUS　　　　　　　　It is a mind

117

III.1

That shall remain a poison where it is,
Not poison any further.

CORIOLANUS                    Shall remain!
Hear you this Triton of the minnows? Mark you
His absolute 'shall'?

COMINIUS                    'Twas from the canon.

CORIOLANUS                                        'Shall'!
O good but most unwise patricians! Why,
You grave but reckless Senators, have you thus
Given Hydra here to choose an officer
That with his peremptory 'shall', being but
The horn and noise o'th'monster's, wants not spirit
To say he'll turn your current in a ditch
And make your channel his? If he have power,
Then vail your ignorance; if none, awake
Your dangerous lenity. If you are learned,
Be not as common fools; if you are not,
Let them have cushions by you. You are plebeians
If they be senators; and they are no less
When, both your voices blended, the great'st taste
Most palates theirs. They choose their magistrate;
And such a one as he, who puts his 'shall',
His popular 'shall', against a graver bench
Than ever frowned in Greece. By Jove himself,
It makes the consuls base! And my soul aches
To know, when two authorities are up,
Neither supreme, how soon confusion
May enter 'twixt the gap of both and take
The one by th'other.

COMINIUS                    Well, on to th'market-place.

CORIOLANUS
Whoever gave that counsel to give forth
The corn o'th'storehouse gratis, as 'twas used
Sometime in Greece –

MENENIUS                    Well, well, no more of that.

CORIOLANUS

Though there the people had more absolute power –
I say they nourished disobedience, fed
The ruin of the state.

BRUTUS                    Why shall the people give
One that speaks thus their voice?

CORIOLANUS                    I'll give my reasons,
More worthier than their voices. They know the corn          120
Was not our recompense, resting well assured
They ne'er did service for't. Being pressed to th'war,
Even when the navel of the state was touched,
They would not thread the gates. This kind of service
Did not deserve corn gratis. Being i'th'war,
Their mutinies and revolts, wherein they showed
Most valour, spoke not for them. Th'accusation
Which they have often made against the Senate,
All cause unborn, could never be the native
Of our so frank donation. Well, what then?          130
How shall this bosom multiplied digest
The Senate's courtesy? Let deeds express
What's like to be their words: 'We did request it;
We are the greater poll, and in true fear
They gave us our demands.' Thus we debase
The nature of our seats, and make the rabble
Call our cares fears; which will in time
Break ope the locks o'th'Senate and bring in
The crows to peck the eagles.

MENENIUS                    Come, enough.

BRUTUS

Enough, with over measure.          No, take more.

CORIOLANUS                    No, take more.          140
What may be sworn by, both divine and human,
Seal what I end withal! This double worship,

III.1

Where one part does disdain with cause, the other
Insult without all reason; where gentry, title, wisdom,
Cannot conclude but by the yea and no
Of general ignorance – it must omit
Real necessities, and give way the while
To unstable slightness. Purpose so barred, it follows
Nothing is done to purpose. Therefore, beseech you –
You that will be less fearful than discreet, 150
That love the fundamental part of state
More than you doubt the change on't, that prefer
A noble life before a long, and wish
To jump a body with a dangerous physic
That's sure of death without it – at once pluck out
The multitudinous tongue, let them not lick
The sweet which is their poison. Your dishonour
Mangles true judgement, and bereaves the state
Of that integrity which should become't,
Not having the power to do the good it would 160
For th'ill which doth control't.

BRUTUS                                    'Has said enough.

SICINIUS

'Has spoken like a traitor and shall answer
As traitors do.

CORIOLANUS   Thou wretch, despite o'erwhelm thee!
What should the people do with these bald Tribunes,
On whom depending, their obedience fails
To th'greater bench? In a rebellion,
When what's not meet, but what must be, was law,
Then were they chosen. In a better hour
Let what is meet be said it must be meet,
And throw their power i'th'dust. 170

BRUTUS

Manifest treason!

SICINIUS                   This a Consul? No.

120

BRUTUS
The Aediles, ho!

*Enter an Aedile*

Let him be apprehended.

SICINIUS
Go call the people, (*Exit Aedile*) in whose name myself
Attach thee as a traitorous innovator,
A foe to th'public weal. Obey, I charge thee,
And follow to thine answer.

CORIOLANUS                    Hence, old goat!

PATRICIANS
We'll surety him.

COMINIUS                    Aged sir, hands off.

CORIOLANUS
Hence, rotten thing! or I shall shake thy bones
Out of thy garments.

SICINIUS                    Help, ye citizens!

*Enter a rabble of Plebeians, with the Aediles*

MENENIUS
On both sides more respect.                                    180

SICINIUS
Here's he that would take from you all your power.

BRUTUS Seize him, Aediles!

PLEBEIANS Down with him, down with him!

SECOND SENATOR Weapons, weapons, weapons!

*They all bustle about Coriolanus*

ALL (*shouting confusedly*)
Tribunes! Patricians! Citizens! What ho!
Sicinius! Brutus! Coriolanus! Citizens!

MENENIUS
Peace, peace, peace! Stay, hold, peace!
What is about to be? I am out of breath.
Confusion's near. I cannot speak. You Tribunes
To th'People – Coriolanus, patience! –                        190

Speak, good Sicinius.

SICINIUS                    Hear me, people. Peace!

PLEBEIANS

Let's hear our Tribune. Peace! Speak, speak, speak.

SICINIUS

You are at point to lose your liberties.

Martius would have all from you, Martius,

Whom late you have named for consul.

MENENIUS                              Fie, fie, fie!

This is the way to kindle, not to quench.

FIRST SENATOR

To unbuild the city and to lay all flat.

SICINIUS

What is the city but the people?

PLEBEIANS                         True,

The people are the city.

BRUTUS

200     By the consent of all we were established

The people's magistrates.

PLEBEIANS                   You so remain.

MENENIUS

And so are like to do.

COMINIUS

That is the way to lay the city flat,

To bring the roof to the foundation,

And bury all which yet distinctly ranges

In heaps and piles of ruin.

SICINIUS                   This deserves death.

BRUTUS

Or let us stand to our authority,

Or let us lose it. We do here pronounce,

Upon the part o'th'people, in whose power

210     We were elected theirs, Martius is worthy

Of present death.

SICINIUS          Therefore lay hold of him;
  Bear him to th'rock Tarpeian, and from thence
  Into destruction cast him.

BRUTUS            Aediles, seize him.

PLEBEIANS
  Yield, Martius, yield.

MENENIUS         Hear me one word.
  Beseech you, Tribunes, hear me but a word.

AEDILES
  Peace, peace!

MENENIUS (*to Brutus*)
  Be that you seem, truly your country's friend,
  And temperately proceed to what you would
  Thus violently redress.

BRUTUS           Sir, those cold ways,
  That seem like prudent helps, are very poisonous     220
  Where the disease is violent. Lay hands upon him
  And bear him to the rock.

    *Coriolanus draws his sword*

CORIOLANUS        No, I'll die here.
  There's some among you have beheld me fighting;
  Come, try upon yourselves what you have seen me.

MENENIUS
  Down with that sword! Tribunes, withdraw awhile.

BRUTUS
  Lay hands upon him.

MENENIUS        Help Martius, help,
  You that be noble, help him, young and old!

PLEBEIANS Down with him, down with him!

    *In this mutiny the Tribunes, the Aediles, and the
    people are beat in*

MENENIUS
  Go, get you to your house! Be gone, away!
  All will be naught else.

SECOND SENATOR          Get you gone.

230 CORIOLANUS                              Stand fast!
We have as many friends as enemies.

MENENIUS
Shall it be put to that?

FIRST SENATOR          The gods forbid!
I prithee, noble friend, home to thy house;
Leave us to cure this cause.

MENENIUS                              For 'tis a sore upon us
You cannot tent yourself. Be gone, beseech you.

COMINIUS
Come, sir, along with us.

CORIOLANUS
I would they were barbarians, as they are,
Though in Rome littered; not Romans, as they are not,
Though calved i'th'porch o'th'Capitol.

MENENIUS                              Be gone.

240 Put not your worthy rage into your tongue.
One time will owe another.

CORIOLANUS                    On fair ground
I could beat forty of them.

MENENIUS                    I could myself
Take up a brace o'th'best of them; yea, the two
Tribunes.

COMINIUS
But now 'tis odds beyond arithmetic,
And manhood is called foolery when it stands
Against a falling fabric. Will you hence
Before the tag return, whose rage doth rend
Like interrupted waters, and o'erbear
What they are used to bear?

MENENIUS                    Pray you be gone.

250 I'll try whether my old wit be in request
With those that have but little. This must be patched

124

With cloth of any colour.

COMINIUS                    Nay, come away.

*Exeunt Coriolanus and Cominius*

PATRICIAN

This man has marred his fortune.

MENENIUS

His nature is too noble for the world.
He would not flatter Neptune for his trident,
Or Jove for's power to thunder. His heart's his mouth.
What his breast forges, that his tongue must vent,
And, being angry, does forget that ever
He heard the name of death.

*A noise within*

Here's goodly work!

PATRICIAN               I would they were a-bed!          260

MENENIUS

I would they were in Tiber! What the vengeance,
Could he not speak 'em fair?

*Enter Brutus and Sicinius, with the rabble again*

SICINIUS               Where is this viper
That would depopulate the city and
Be every man himself?

MENENIUS               You worthy Tribunes –

SICINIUS

He shall be thrown down the Tarpeian rock
With rigorous hands. He hath resisted law,
And therefore law shall scorn him further trial
Than the severity of the public power,
Which he so sets at naught.

FIRST CITIZEN               He shall well know
The noble Tribunes are the people's mouths,          270
And we their hands.

PLEBEIANS          He shall, sure on't.

MENENIUS               Sir, sir –

125

**III.1**

SICINIUS
Peace!

MENENIUS
Do not cry havoc, where you should but hunt
With modest warrant.

SICINIUS                    Sir, how comes't that you
Have holp to make this rescue?

MENENIUS                         Hear me speak.
As I do know the Consul's worthiness,
So can I name his faults.

SICINIUS                    Consul! What Consul?

MENENIUS
The Consul Coriolanus.

BRUTUS                He Consul!

PLEBEIANS No, no, no, no, no.

MENENIUS
280    If, by the Tribunes' leave and yours, good people,
    I may be heard, I would crave a word or two,
    The which shall turn you to no further harm
    Than so much loss of time.

SICINIUS                    Speak briefly then,
    For we are peremptory to dispatch
    This viperous traitor. To eject him hence
    Were but our danger, and to keep him here
    Our certain death. Therefore it is decreed
    He dies tonight.

MENENIUS        Now the good gods forbid
    That our renownèd Rome, whose gratitude
290    Towards her deservèd children is enrolled
    In Jove's own book, like an unnatural dam
    Should now eat up her own!

SICINIUS
He's a disease that must be cut away.

MENENIUS
O, he's a limb that has but a disease –

126

Mortal, to cut it off; to cure it, easy.
What has he done to Rome that's worthy death?
Killing our enemies, the blood he hath lost –
Which I dare vouch is more than that he hath
By many an ounce – he dropped it for his country;
And what is left, to lose it by his country               300
Were to us all that do't and suffer it
A brand to th'end o'th'world.

SICINIUS                     This is clean kam.

BRUTUS
Merely awry. When he did love his country,
It honoured him.

SICINIUS           The service of the foot,
Being once gangrened, is not then respected
For what before it was.

BRUTUS                   We'll hear no more.
Pursue him to his house and pluck him thence,
Lest his infection, being of catching nature,
Spread further.

MENENIUS         One word more, one word!
This tiger-footed rage, when it shall find               310
The harm of unscanned swiftness, will too late
Tie leaden pounds to's heels. Proceed by process,
Lest parties – as he is beloved – break out
And sack great Rome with Romans.

BRUTUS                           If it were so –

SICINIUS
What do ye talk?
Have we not had a taste of his obedience?
Our Aediles smote? Ourselves resisted? Come!

MENENIUS
Consider this. He has been bred i'th'wars
Since 'a could draw a sword, and is ill schooled
In bolted language. Meal and bran together               320
He throws without distinction. Give me leave,

I'll go to him and undertake to bring him
Where he shall answer by a lawful form,
In peace, to his utmost peril.

FIRST SENATOR                    Noble Tribunes,
It is the humane way. The other course
Will prove too bloody, and the end of it
Unknown to the beginning.

SICINIUS                    Noble Menenius,
Be you then as the people's officer.
Masters, lay down your weapons.

BRUTUS                              Go not home.

SICINIUS

330   Meet on the market-place. We'll attend you there;
Where, if you bring not Martius, we'll proceed
In our first way.

MENENIUS          I'll bring him to you.
(to the Senators) Let me desire your company. He must
    come,
Or what is worst will follow.

FIRST SENATOR               Pray you let's to him.

*Exeunt*


III.2          *Enter Coriolanus, with Nobles*

CORIOLANUS

Let them pull all about mine ears, present me
Death on the wheel or at wild horses' heels,
Or pile ten hills on the Tarpeian rock,
That the precipitation might down stretch
Below the beam of sight, yet will I still
Be thus to them.

NOBLE               You do the nobler.

CORIOLANUS

I muse my mother
Does not approve me further, who was wont

128

To call them woollen vassals, things created
To buy and sell with groats, to show bare heads          10
In congregations, to yawn, be still and wonder,
When one but of my ordinance stood up
To speak of peace or war.

    *Enter Volumnia*

                I talk of you:
Why did you wish me milder? Would you have me
False to my nature? Rather say I play
The man I am.

VOLUMNIA        O, sir, sir, sir,
I would have had you put your power well on
Before you had worn it out.

CORIOLANUS           Let go.

VOLUMNIA
You might have been enough the man you are
With striving less to be so. Lesser had been          20
The crossings of your dispositions, if
You had not showed them how ye were disposed
Ere they lacked power to cross you.

CORIOLANUS           Let them hang!

VOLUMNIA
Ay, and burn too!

    *Enter Menenius, with the Senators*

MENENIUS
Come, come, you have been too rough, something too
    rough.
You must return and mend it.

FIRST SENATOR        There's no remedy,
Unless, by not so doing, our good city
Cleave in the midst and perish.

VOLUMNIA           Pray be counselled.
I have a heart as little apt as yours,
But yet a brain that leads my use of anger          30

129

To better vantage.

MENENIUS                Well said, noble woman!
Before he should thus stoop to th'heart, but that
The violent fit o'th'time craves it as physic
For the whole state, I would put mine armour on,
Which I can scarcely bear.

CORIOLANUS                What must I do?

MENENIUS
Return to th'Tribunes.

CORIOLANUS                Well, what then? What then?

MENENIUS
Repent what you have spoke.

CORIOLANUS
For them! I cannot do it to the gods.
Must I then do't to them?

VOLUMNIA                You are too absolute,
40    Though therein you can never be too noble.
But when extremities speak, I have heard you say,
Honour and policy, like unsevered friends,
I'th'war do grow together. Grant that, and tell me
In peace what each of them by th'other lose
That they combine not there.

CORIOLANUS                Tush, tush!

MENENIUS                            A good demand.

VOLUMNIA
If it be honour in your wars to seem
The same you are not, which for your best ends
You adopt your policy, how is it less or worse
That it shall hold companionship in peace
50    With honour as in war, since that to both
It stands in like request?

CORIOLANUS                Why force you this?

VOLUMNIA
Because that now it lies you on to speak

130

To th'people, not by your own instruction,
Nor by th'matter which your heart prompts you,
But with such words that are but roted in
Your tongue, though but bastards and syllables
Of no allowance to your bosom's truth.
Now this no more dishonours you at all
Than to take in a town with gentle words,
Which else would put you to your fortune and          60
The hazard of much blood.
I would dissemble with my nature where
My fortunes and my friends at stake required
I should do so in honour. I am in this
Your wife, your son, these Senators, the nobles;
And you will rather show our general louts
How you can frown, than spend a fawn upon 'em
For the inheritance of their loves and safeguard
Of what that want might ruin.

MENENIUS                    Noble lady!
– Come, go with us, speak fair. You may salve so,          70
Not what is dangerous present, but the loss
Of what is past.

VOLUMNIA          I prithee now, my son,
Go to them with this bonnet in thy hand;
And thus far having stretched it – here be with them –
Thy knee bussing the stones – for in such business
Action is eloquence, and the eyes of th'ignorant
More learnèd than the ears – waving thy head,
With often thus correcting thy stout heart,
Now humble as the ripest mulberry
That will not hold the handling, say to them          80
Thou art their soldier, and being bred in broils
Hast not the soft way which, thou dost confess,
Were fit for thee to use as they to claim,
In asking their good loves; but thou wilt frame

Thyself, forsooth, hereafter theirs, so far
As thou hast power and person.

MENENIUS                    This but done
Even as she speaks, why, their hearts were yours.
For they have pardons, being asked, as free
As words to little purpose.

VOLUMNIA                    Prithee now,
Go, and be ruled; although I know thou hadst rather
Follow thine enemy in a fiery gulf
Than flatter him in a bower.

        *Enter Cominius*

                                        Here is Cominius.

COMINIUS
I have been i'th'market-place; and, sir, 'tis fit
You make strong party, or defend yourself
By calmness or by absence. All's in anger.

MENENIUS
Only fair speech.

COMINIUS            I think 'twill serve, if he
Can thereto frame his spirit.

VOLUMNIA                    He must, and will.
Prithee now, say you will, and go about it.

CORIOLANUS
Must I go show them my unbarbed sconce? Must I
With my base tongue give to my noble heart
A lie that it must bear? Well, I will do't.
Yet, were there but this single plot to lose,
This mould of Martius, they to dust should grind it
And throw't against the wind. To th'market-place!
You have put me now to such a part which never
I shall discharge to th'life.

COMINIUS                    Come, come, we'll prompt you.

VOLUMNIA
I prithee now, sweet son, as thou hast said

132

My praises made thee first a soldier, so,
To have my praise for this, perform a part
Thou hast not done before.

CORIOLANUS                    Well, I must do't.                    110
Away, my disposition, and possess me
Some harlot's spirit! My throat of war be turned,
Which choired with my drum, into a pipe
Small as an eunuch or the virgin voice
That babies lulls asleep! The smiles of knaves
Tent in my cheeks, and schoolboys' tears take up
The glasses of my sight! A beggar's tongue
Make motion through my lips, and my armed knees,
Who bowed but in my stirrup, bend like his
That hath received an alms! I will not do't,                    120
Lest I surcease to honour mine own truth
And by my body's action teach my mind
A most inherent baseness.

VOLUMNIA                    At thy choice, then.
To beg of thee, it is my more dishonour
Than thou of them. Come all to ruin. Let
Thy mother rather feel thy pride than fear
Thy dangerous stoutness, for I mock at death
With as big heart as thou. Do as thou list.
Thy valiantness was mine, thou suck'dst it from me,
But owe thy pride thyself.

CORIOLANUS                    Pray be content.                    130
Mother, I am going to the market-place.
Chide me no more. I'll mountebank their loves,
Cog their hearts from them, and come home beloved
Of all the trades in Rome. Look, I am going.
Commend me to my wife. I'll return consul,
Or never trust to what my tongue can do
I'th'way of flattery further.

VOLUMNIA                    Do your will. *Exit Volumnia*

COMINIUS

    Away! The Tribunes do attend you. Arm yourself
    To answer mildly; for they are prepared
140    With accusations, as I hear, more strong
    Than are upon you yet.

CORIOLANUS

    The word is 'mildly'. Pray you let us go.
    Let them accuse me by invention, I
    Will answer in mine honour.

MENENIUS                   Ay, but mildly.

CORIOLANUS

    Well, mildly be it then – mildly.          *Exeunt*


III.3        *Enter Sicinius and Brutus*

BRUTUS

    In this point charge him home, that he affects
    Tyrannical power. If he evade us there,
    Enforce him with his envy to the people,
    And that the spoil got on the Antiates
    Was ne'er distributed.

          *Enter an Aedile*

                    What, will he come?

AEDILE

    He's coming.

BRUTUS        How accompanied?

AEDILE

    With old Menenius and those senators
    That always favoured him.

SICINIUS             Have you a catalogue
    Of all the voices that we have procured,
10    Set down by th'poll?

AEDILE          I have; 'tis ready.

SICINIUS

  Have you collected them by tribes?

AEDILE                           I have.

SICINIUS

  Assemble presently the people hither.

  And when they hear me say 'It shall be so

  I'th'right and strength o'th'commons' be it either

  For death, for fine, or banishment, then let them,

  If I say 'Fine', cry 'Fine!', if 'Death', cry 'Death!'

  Insisting on the old prerogative

  And power i'th'truth o'th'cause.

AEDILE                 I shall inform them.

BRUTUS

  And when such time they have begun to cry,

  Let them not cease, but with a din confused         20

  Enforce the present execution

  Of what we chance to sentence.

AEDILE               Very well.

SICINIUS

  Make them be strong, and ready for this hint

  When we shall hap to give't them.

BRUTUS            Go about it. *Exit Aedile*

  Put him to choler straight. He hath been used

  Ever to conquer and to have his worth

  Of contradiction. Being once chafed, he cannot

  Be reined again to temperance, then he speaks

  What's in his heart, and that is there which looks

  With us to break his neck.

      *Enter Coriolanus, Menenius, and Cominius, with others*

SICINIUS          Well, here he comes.       30

MENENIUS

  Calmly, I do beseech you.

CORIOLANUS

  Ay, as an hostler, that for th'poorest piece

Will bear the knave by th'volume. (*Aloud*) Th'honoured
    gods
Keep Rome in safety and the chairs of justice
Supplied with worthy men! Plant love among's!
Throng our large temples with the shows of peace,
And not our streets with war!

**FIRST SENATOR**              Amen, amen.

**MENENIUS**

A noble wish.

    *Enter the Aedile, with the Plebeians*

**SICINIUS**

Draw near, ye people.

**AEDILE**

40   List to your Tribunes. Audience! Peace, I say!

**CORIOLANUS**

First, hear me speak.

**BOTH TRIBUNES**      Well, say. Peace ho!

**CORIOLANUS**

Shall I be charged no further than this present?
Must all determine here?

**SICINIUS**             I do demand
If you submit you to the people's voices,
Allow their officers, and are content
To suffer lawful censure for such faults
As shall be proved upon you?

**CORIOLANUS**            I am content.

**MENENIUS**

Lo, citizens, he says he is content.
The warlike service he has done, consider. Think
50  Upon the wounds his body bears, which show
Like graves i'th'holy churchyard.

**CORIOLANUS**         Scratches with briers,
Scars to move laughter only.

**MENENIUS**            Consider further,

That when he speaks not like a citizen,
You find him like a soldier. Do not take
His rougher accents for malicious sounds,
But, as I say, such as become a soldier
Rather than envy you.

COMINIUS                Well, well, no more.

CORIOLANUS
What is the matter
That being passed for consul with full voice,
I am so dishonoured that the very hour
You take it off again?

SICINIUS                Answer to us.

CORIOLANUS
Say, then. 'Tis true, I ought so.

SICINIUS
We charge you that you have contrived to take
From Rome all seasoned office and to wind
Yourself into a power tyrannical,
For which you are a traitor to the people.

CORIOLANUS
How – traitor?

MENENIUS        Nay, temperately! Your promise.

CORIOLANUS
The fires i'th'lowest hell fold in the people!
Call me their traitor, thou injurious Tribune!
Within thine eyes sat twenty thousand deaths,     70
In thy hands clutched as many millions, in
Thy lying tongue both numbers, I would say
'Thou liest' unto thee with a voice as free
As I do pray the gods.

SICINIUS                Mark you this, people?

PLEBEIANS
To th'rock, to th'rock with him!

SICINIUS                        Peace!

137

III.3

We need not put new matter to his charge.
What you have seen him do and heard him speak,
Beating your officers, cursing yourselves,
Opposing laws with strokes, and here defying
80 Those whose great power must try him – even this,
So criminal and in such capital kind,
Deserves th'extremest death.

BRUTUS                                    But since he hath
Served well for Rome –

CORIOLANUS                  What do you prate of service?

BRUTUS
I talk of that that know it.

CORIOLANUS
You!

MENENIUS
Is this the promise that you made your mother?

COMINIUS
Know, I pray you –

CORIOLANUS          I'll know no further.
Let them pronounce the steep Tarpeian death,
Vagabond exile, flaying, pent to linger
90 But with a grain a day, I would not buy
Their mercy at the price of one fair word,
Nor check my courage for what they can give,
To have't with saying 'Good morrow'.

SICINIUS                                    For that he has –
As much as in him lies – from time to time
Envied against the people, seeking means
To pluck away their power, as now at last
Given hostile strokes, and that not in the presence
Of dreaded justice, but on the ministers
That doth distribute it – in the name o'th'people
100 And in the power of us the Tribunes, we,
Even from this instant, banish him our city,

138

In peril of precipitation
From off the rock Tarpeian, never more
To enter our Rome gates. I'th'people's name,
I say it shall be so.

PLEBEIANS
It shall be so, it shall be so! Let him away!
He's banished, and it shall be so.

COMINIUS
Hear me, my masters and my common friends –

SICINIUS
He's sentenced. No more hearing.

COMINIUS                         Let me speak.
I have been Consul, and can show for Rome          110
Her enemies' marks upon me. I do love
My country's good with a respect more tender,
More holy and profound, than mine own life,
My dear wife's estimate, her womb's increase
And treasure of my loins. Then if I would
Speak that –

SICINIUS       We know your drift. Speak what?

BRUTUS
There's no more to be said, but he is banished
As enemy to the people and his country.
It shall be so.

PLEBEIANS       It shall be so, it shall be so!

CORIOLANUS
You common cry of curs, whose breath I hate        120
As reek o'th'rotten fens, whose loves I prize
As the dead carcasses of unburied men
That do corrupt my air – I banish you.
And here remain with your uncertainty!
Let every feeble rumour shake your hearts;
Your enemies, with nodding of their plumes,
Fan you into despair! Have the power still

To banish your defenders, till at length
Your ignorance – which finds not till it feels,
130   Making but reservation of yourselves
Still your own foes – deliver you
As most abated captives to some nation
That won you without blows! Despising
For you the city, thus I turn my back.
There is a world elsewhere.     *Exeunt Coriolanus,*
        *Cominius, Menenius, with the other Patricians*

AEDILE
The people's enemy is gone, is gone!

PLEBEIANS
Our enemy is banished, he is gone! Hoo-oo!
    *They all shout, and throw up their caps*

SICINIUS
Go see him out at gates, and follow him
As he hath followed you, with all despite;
140   Give him deserved vexation. Let a guard
Attend us through the city.

PLEBEIANS
Come, come, let's see him out at gates, come!
The gods preserve our noble Tribunes! Come! *Exeunt*

IV.1     *Enter Coriolanus, Volumnia, Virgilia, Menenius,*
     *Cominius, with the young Nobility of Rome*

CORIOLANUS
Come, leave your tears. A brief farewell. The beast
With many heads butts me away. Nay, mother,
Where is your ancient courage? You were used
To say extremities was the trier of spirits;

That common chances common men could bear;
That when the sea was calm all boats alike
Showed mastership in floating; fortune's blows
When most struck home, being gentle wounded craves
A noble cunning. You were used to load me
With precepts that would make invincible                    10
The heart that conned them.

VIRGILIA

O heavens! O heavens!

CORIOLANUS                    Nay, I prithee, woman –

VOLUMNIA

Now the red pestilence strike all trades in Rome,
And occupations perish!

CORIOLANUS                    What, what, what!
I shall be loved when I am lacked. Nay, mother,
Resume that spirit when you were wont to say,
If you had been the wife of Hercules,
Six of his labours you'd have done, and saved
Your husband so much sweat. Cominius,
Droop not. Adieu. Farewell, my wife, my mother.          20
I'll do well yet. Thou old and true Menenius,
Thy tears are salter than a younger man's
And venomous to thine eyes. My sometime general,
I have seen thee stern, and thou hast oft beheld
Heart-hardening spectacles. Tell these sad women
'Tis fond to wail inevitable strokes,
As 'tis to laugh at 'em. My mother, you wot well
My hazards still have been your solace, and
Believe't not lightly – though I go alone,
Like to a lonely dragon that his fen                        30
Makes feared and talked of more than seen – your son
Will or exceed the common or be caught
With cautelous baits and practice.

VOLUMNIA                    My first son,

## IV.1

Whither wilt thou go? Take good Cominius
With thee awhile. Determine on some course
More than a wild exposture to each chance
That starts i'th'way before thee.

VIRGILIA                              O the gods!

COMINIUS

I'll follow thee a month, devise with thee
Where thou shalt rest, that thou mayst hear of us
40      And we of thee. So, if the time thrust forth
A cause for thy repeal, we shall not send
O'er the vast world to seek a single man,
And lose advantage, which doth ever cool
I'th'absence of the needer.

CORIOLANUS                          Fare ye well.
Thou hast years upon thee, and thou art too full
Of the wars' surfeits to go rove with one
That's yet unbruised. Bring me but out at gate.
Come, my sweet wife, my dearest mother, and
My friends of noble touch, when I am forth,
50      Bid me farewell, and smile. I pray you come.
While I remain above the ground you shall
Hear from me still, and never of me aught
But what is like me formerly.

MENENIUS                          That's worthily
As any ear can hear. Come, let's not weep.
If I could shake off but one seven years
From these old arms and legs, by the good gods,
I'd with thee every foot.

CORIOLANUS                          Give me thy hand.
Come.                                                      *Exeunt*

142

*Enter the two Tribunes, Sicinius and Brutus, with the* IV.2
*Aedile*

SICINIUS

Bid them all home. He's gone, and we'll no further.
The nobility are vexed, whom we see have sided
In his behalf.

*will not push our luck*
*} suggestion of fear?*

BRUTUS          Now we have shown our power,
Let us seem humbler after it is done
Than when it was a-doing.

SICINIUS                    Bid them home.
Say their great enemy is gone, and they
Stand in their ancient strength.

BRUTUS                         Dismiss them home.

*Exit Aedile*

Here comes his mother.
*Enter Volumnia, Virgilia, and Menenius*

SICINIUS                    Let's not meet her.

BRUTUS                                        Why?

SICINIUS

They say she's mad.

BRUTUS

They have ta'en note of us. Keep on your way.          10

*short converse suggests agitation*

VOLUMNIA

O, y'are well met. Th'hoarded plague o'th'gods
Requite your love!

*sarcasm*

MENENIUS          Peace, peace, be not so loud.

VOLUMNIA

If that I could for weeping, you should hear –
Nay, and you shall hear some. (*To Brutus*) Will you be
gone?

VIRGILIA (*to Sicinius*)

You shall stay too. I would I had the power
To say so to my husband.

SICINIUS                    Are you mankind?

*mad*

143

IV.2

*contempt*

**VOLUMNIA**
Ay, fool, is that a shame? Note but this, fool:
Was not a man my father? Hadst thou foxship
To banish him that struck more blows for Rome
20    Than thou hast spoken words?

**SICINIUS**                    O blessed heavens!

**VOLUMNIA**
More noble blows than ever thou wise words,
And for Rome's good. I'll tell thee what – yet go.
Nay, but thou shalt stay too. I would my son

*away from the plebs*

Were in Arabia, and thy tribe before him,
His good sword in his hand.

**SICINIUS**                    What then?

**VIRGILIA**                              What then!
He'd make an end of thy posterity.

**VOLUMNIA**
Bastards and all.
Good man, the wounds that he does bear for Rome!

**MENENIUS**
Come, come, peace.

**SICINIUS**
30    I would he had continued to his country
As he began, and not unknit himself

*untie*

The noble knot he made.

*band of service*

**BRUTUS**                    I would he had.

**VOLUMNIA**
'I would he had'! 'Twas you incensed the rabble –

*feminine of Coriolanus's 'curs'*

Cats that can judge as fitly of his worth
As I can of those mysteries which heaven
Will not have earth to know.

**BRUTUS**                    Pray, let's go.

**VOLUMNIA**
Now, pray, sir, get you gone.

*irony*

You have done a brave deed. Ere you go, hear this:

144

As far as doth the Capitol exceed
The meanest house in Rome, so far my son –           40
This lady's husband here, this, do you see? –
Whom you have banished does exceed you all.

BRUTUS
Well, well, we'll leave you.

SICINIUS                    Why stay we to be baited
With one that wants her wits?           *Exeunt Tribunes*

VOLUMNIA                    Take my prayers with you.
I would the gods had nothing else to do
But to confirm my curses. Could I meet 'em
But once a day, it would unclog my heart
Of what lies heavy to't.

MENENIUS                    You have told them home,          *rebuked them thoroughly*
And, by my troth, you have cause. You'll sup with me?

VOLUMNIA
Anger's my meat. I sup upon myself,           50
And so shall starve with feeding. (*To Virgilia*) Come,
      let's go.                          *wimpering*
Leave this faint puling and lament as I do,
In anger, Juno-like. Come, come, come.
                              *chief goddess of*
                              *Exeunt Volumnia and Virgilia*
MENENIUS                    *the Romans*
Fie, fie, fie.                                    *Exit*

*Scene brings back the Volsces. Indicates*
*the trend of things. We learn of Volscean*
         *Enter a Roman and a Volsce*           IV.3    *attack*
                                                        *on Rome.*
ROMAN I know you well, sir, and you know me. Your
   name, I think, is Adrian.                            *Re-introd.*
VOLSCE It is so, sir. Truly, I have forgot you.         *theme*
         *I am in your pay*
ROMAN I am a Roman; and my services are, as you are,   *of treachery:*
   against 'em. Know you me yet?
VOLSCE Nicanor, no?                                     *— reference*
ROMAN The same, sir.
                                                        *Act 1, Scene 10*
                    145                                 *(line 27)*

VOLSCE You had more beard when I last saw you, but your favour is well approved by your tongue. What's the news in Rome? I have a note from the Volscian state to find you out there. You have well saved me a day's journey.

ROMAN There hath been in Rome strange insurrections: the people against the senators, patricians and nobles.

VOLSCE Hath been? Is it ended then? Our state thinks not so. They are in a most warlike preparation, and hope to come upon them in the heat of their division.

ROMAN The main blaze of it is past, but a small thing would make it flame again. For the nobles receive so to heart the banishment of that worthy Coriolanus that they are in a ripe aptness to take all power from the people and to pluck from them their tribunes for ever. This lies glowing, I can tell you, and is almost mature for the violent breaking out.

VOLSCE Coriolanus banished?

ROMAN Banished, sir.

VOLSCE You will be welcome with this intelligence, Nicanor.

ROMAN The day serves well for them now. I have heard it said the fittest time to corrupt a man's wife is when she's fallen out with her husband. Your noble Tullus Aufidius will appear well in these wars, his great opposer, Coriolanus, being now in no request of his country.

VOLSCE He cannot choose. I am most fortunate thus accidentally to encounter you. You have ended my business, and I will merrily accompany you home.

ROMAN I shall between this and supper tell you most strange things from Rome, all tending to the good of their adversaries. Have you an army ready, say you?

VOLSCE A most royal one. The centurions and their charges distinctly billeted, already in th'entertainment, and to be on foot at an hour's warning.

146

ROMAN I am joyful to hear of their readiness, and am the
man, I think, that shall set them in present action. So,
sir, heartily well met, and most glad of your company.

VOLSCE You take my part from me, sir. I have the most
cause to be glad of yours.

ROMAN Well, let us go together.                    *Exeunt*

*Taken almost wholly from North*

*Enter Coriolanus in mean apparel, disguised and muffled*  IV.4

CORIOLANUS

A goodly city is this Antium. City,
'Tis I that made thy widows. Many an heir
Of these fair edifices 'fore my wars
Have I heard groan and drop. Then know me not,
Lest that thy wives with spits and boys with stones
In puny battle slay me.

*Justifying his disguise*

*in the face of my attacks.*

        *Enter a Citizen*

                    Save you, sir.

CITIZEN

And you.

CORIOLANUS Direct me, if it be your will,
Where great Aufidius lies. Is he in Antium?

*pun?*

CITIZEN

He is, and feasts the nobles of the state
At his house this night.

CORIOLANUS                    Which is his house, beseech you?  10

CITIZEN

This here before you.

CORIOLANUS                    Thank you, sir. Farewell.

                              *Exit Citizen*

*fickle changes*

O world, thy slippery turns! Friends now fast sworn,
Whose double bosoms seems to wear one heart,
Whose hours, whose bed, whose meal and exercise
Are still together, who twin, as 'twere, in love

*inseparable friends*

147

*The main purpose of the scene is to show Coriolanus's determination at Antium as he had in Rome.*

*This soliloquy is not reflection. He is not explaining his decision, he does not know why he reached his decision.*

*It is the justification for the decision*

Unseparable, shall within this hour,
On a dissension of a doit, break out
To bitterest enmity. So fellest foes,
Whose passions and whose plots have broke their sleep
20  To take the one the other, by some chance,
Some trick not worth an egg, shall grow dear friends
And interjoin their issues. So with me.
My birthplace hate I, and my love's upon
This enemy town. I'll enter. If he slay me,
He does fair justice. If he give me way,
I'll do his country service.                    *Exit*

*paradox of hating his birthplace loving his enemies town*

*out of character*

*Aufidius takes Coriolanus in.*

**IV.5**                    *Music plays. Enter a Servingman*

*The scene is based on Plutarch. Up to Coriolanus' large speech onward is pure Plutarch.*

FIRST SERVINGMAN Wine, wine, wine! What service is
here? I think our fellows are asleep.          *Exit*
                *Enter another Servingman*

SECOND SERVINGMAN Where's Cotus? My master calls
for him. Cotus!                                *Exit*
                *Enter Coriolanus*

CORIOLANUS
A goodly house. The feast smells well, but I
Appear not like a guest.
                *Enter the First Servingman*

FIRST SERVINGMAN What would you have, friend?
Whence are you? Here's no place for you. Pray go to the
door.                                          *Exit*

*irony*

CORIOLANUS
10  I have deserved no better entertainment
In being Coriolanus.

*an aside*

                *Enter Second Servingman*

SECOND SERVINGMAN Whence are you, sir? Has the
porter his eyes in his head that he gives entrance to such
companions? Pray get you out.

CORIOLANUS Away!

SECOND SERVINGMAN Away? Get you away.

CORIOLANUS Now th' art troublesome.

SECOND SERVINGMAN Are you so brave? I'll have you
talked with anon.

*Enter Third Servingman. The First meets him*

THIRD SERVINGMAN What fellow's this?                    20

FIRST SERVINGMAN A strange one as ever I looked on.
I cannot get him out o'th'house. Prithee call my master
to him.

THIRD SERVINGMAN What have you to do here, fellow?
Pray you avoid the house.

CORIOLANUS
Let me but stand – I will not hurt your hearth.

THIRD SERVINGMAN What are you?

CORIOLANUS A gentleman.

THIRD SERVINGMAN A marvellous poor one.

CORIOLANUS True, so I am.                              30

THIRD SERVINGMAN Pray you, poor gentleman, take up
some other station. Here's no place for you. Pray you
avoid. Come.

CORIOLANUS Follow your function, go and batten on
cold bits.

*He pushes him away from him*

THIRD SERVINGMAN What, you will not? Prithee tell
my master what a strange guest he has here.

SECOND SERVINGMAN And I shall.

*Exit Second Servingman*

THIRD SERVINGMAN Where dwell'st thou?

CORIOLANUS Under the canopy.                           40

THIRD SERVINGMAN Under the canopy?

CORIOLANUS Ay.

THIRD SERVINGMAN Where's that?

CORIOLANUS I'th'city of kites and crows.

THIRD SERVINGMAN I'th'city of kites and crows? What
an ass it is! Then thou dwell'st with daws too?

CORIOLANUS No, I serve not thy master.

THIRD SERVINGMAN How, sir? Do you meddle with my
master?

50 CORIOLANUS Ay, 'tis an honester service than to meddle
with thy mistress. Thou prat'st and prat'st. Serve with
thy trencher. Hence!

*He beats him away from the stage*
*Enter Aufidius with the Second Servingman*

AUFIDIUS Where is this fellow?

SECOND SERVINGMAN Here, sir. I'd have beaten him
like a dog, but for disturbing the lords within.

*Servingmen stand aside*

AUFIDIUS
Whence com'st thou? What wouldst thou? Thy name?
Why speak'st not? Speak, man. What's thy name?

CORIOLANUS (*unmuffling*)                              If, Tullus,
Not yet thou know'st me, and, seeing me, dost not
Think me for the man I am, necessity
60 Commands me name myself.

AUFIDIUS                              What is thy name?

CORIOLANUS
A name unmusical to the Volscians' ears,
And harsh in sound to thine.

AUFIDIUS                              Say, what's thy name?
Thou hast a grim appearance, and thy face
Bears a command in't. Though thy tackle's torn,
Thou show'st a noble vessel. What's thy name?

CORIOLANUS
Prepare thy brow to frown. Know'st thou me yet?

AUFIDIUS
I know thee not. Thy name?

CORIOLANUS
My name is Caius Martius, who hath done

150

To thee particularly and to all the Volsces
Great hurt and mischief; thereto witness may                    70
My surname, Coriolanus. The painful service,
The extreme dangers, and the drops of blood
Shed for my thankless country, are requited
But with that surname – a good memory *— memorial*
And witness of the malice and displeasure
Which thou shouldst bear me. Only that name remains.
The cruelty and envy of the people,
Permitted by our dastard nobles, who            *he is as angry*
Have all forsook me, hath devoured the rest,    *with the*
And suffered me by th'voice of slaves to be     *nobles as*  80
Whooped out of Rome. Now this extremity         *the commoners.*
Hath brought me to thy hearth, not out of hope –
Mistake me not – to save my life; for if
I had feared death, of all men i'th'world
I would have 'voided thee; but in mere spite,   *out of*
To be full quit of those my banishers,
Stand I before thee here. Then if thou hast      *vengeance*
A heart of wreak in thee, that wilt revenge
Thine own particular wrongs and stop those maims  *injuries*
Of shame seen through thy country, speed thee straight  90
And make my misery serve thy turn. So use it
That my revengeful services may prove
As benefits to thee. For I will fight            *= imagery*
Against my cankered country with the spleen
Of all the under fiends. But if so be            *Fiends in hell.*
Thou dar'st not this, and that to prove more fortunes  *try*
Th' art tired, then, in a word, I also am
Longer to live most weary, and present
My throat to thee and to thy ancient malice;
Which not to cut would show thee but a fool,            100
Since I have ever followed thee with hate,
Drawn tuns of blood out of thy country's breast,  *barrels*
And cannot live but by thy shame, unless

It be to do thee service.

AUFIDIUS                        O Martius, Martius!
Each word thou hast spoke hath weeded from my heart
A root of ancient envy. If Jupiter
Should from yond cloud speak divine things,
And say ' 'Tis true', I'd not believe them more
Than thee, all-noble Martius. Let me twine
110   Mine arms about that body, whereagainst
My grainèd ash an hundred times hath broke
And scarred the moon with splinters. Here I clip
The anvil of my sword, and do contest
As hotly and as nobly with thy love
As ever in ambitious strength I did
Contend against thy valour. Know thou first,
I loved the maid I married; never man
Sighed truer breath. But that I see thee here,
Thou noble thing, more dances my rapt heart
120   Than when I first my wedded mistress saw
Bestride my threshold. Why, thou Mars, I tell thee
We have a power on foot, and I had purpose
Once more to hew thy target from thy brawn,
Or lose mine arm for't. Thou hast beat me out
Twelve several times, and I have nightly since
Dreamt of encounters 'twixt thyself and me –
We have been down together in my sleep,
Unbuckling helms, fisting each other's throat –
And waked half dead with nothing. Worthy Martius,
130   Had we no other quarrel else to Rome but that
Thou art thence banished, we would muster all
From twelve to seventy, and pouring war
Into the bowels of ungrateful Rome,
Like a bold flood o'erbear't. O, come, go in,
And take our friendly senators by th'hands,
Who now are here, taking their leaves of me
Who am prepared against your territories,

Though not for Rome itself.

CORIOLANUS                          You bless me, gods!

AUFIDIUS

Therefore, most absolute sir, if thou wilt have
The leading of thine own revenges, take                    140
Th'one half of my commission, and set down –
As best thou art experienced, since thou know'st
Thy country's strength and weakness – thine own ways,
Whether to knock against the gates of Rome,
Or rudely visit them in parts remote
To fright them ere destroy. But come in.
Let me commend thee first to those that shall
Say yea to thy desires. A thousand welcomes!
And more a friend than e'er an enemy;
Yet, Martius, that was much. Your hand. Most welcome!   150

*Exeunt*

*First and Second Servingmen come forward*

FIRST SERVINGMAN Here's a strange alteration!

SECOND SERVINGMAN By my hand, I had thought to
have strucken him with a cudgel, and yet my mind gave
me his clothes made a false report of him.

FIRST SERVINGMAN What an arm he has! He turned me
about with his finger and his thumb as one would set up
a top.

SECOND SERVINGMAN Nay, I knew by his face that
there was something in him. He had, sir, a kind of face,
methought – I cannot tell how to term it.                  160

FIRST SERVINGMAN He had so, looking as it were –
Would I were hanged, but I thought there was more in
him than I could think.

SECOND SERVINGMAN So did I, I'll be sworn. He is
simply the rarest man i'th'world.

FIRST SERVINGMAN I think he is. But a greater soldier
than he you wot one.

SECOND SERVINGMAN Who, my master?

153

FIRST SERVINGMAN Nay, it's no matter for that.

170 SECOND SERVINGMAN Worth six on him.

FIRST SERVINGMAN Nay, not so neither. But I take him
to be the greater soldier.

SECOND SERVINGMAN Faith, look you, one cannot tell
how to say that. For the defence of a town our general
is excellent.

FIRST SERVINGMAN Ay, and for an assault too.

*Enter the Third Servingman*

THIRD SERVINGMAN O slaves, I can tell you news –
news, you rascals!

BOTH What, what, what? Let's partake.

180 THIRD SERVINGMAN I would not be a Roman, of all
nations. I had as lief be a condemned man.

BOTH Wherefore? Wherefore?

THIRD SERVINGMAN Why, here's he that was wont to
thwack our general, Caius Martius.

FIRST SERVINGMAN Why do you say 'thwack our
General'?

THIRD SERVINGMAN I do not say 'thwack our general',
but he was always good enough for him.

SECOND SERVINGMAN Come, we are fellows and friends.
190 He was ever too hard for him, I have heard him say so
himself.

FIRST SERVINGMAN He was too hard for him, directly
to say the truth on't. Before Corioles he scotched him
and notched him like a carbonado.

SECOND SERVINGMAN An he had been cannibally given,
he might have boiled and eaten him too.

FIRST SERVINGMAN But more of thy news!

THIRD SERVINGMAN Why, he is so made on here within
as if he were son and heir to Mars; set at upper end
200 o'th'table; no question asked him by any of the senators
but they stand bald before him. Our general himself

makes a mistress of him, sanctifies himself with's hand,
and turns up the white o'th'eye to his discourse. But the
bottom of the news is, our general is cut i'th'middle and
but one half of what he was yesterday, for the other has
half by the entreaty and grant of the whole table. He'll
go, he says, and sowl the porter of Rome gates by th'ears.
He will mow all down before him, and leave his passage
polled.

SECOND SERVINGMAN And he's as like to do't as any 210
man I can imagine.

THIRD SERVINGMAN Do't! He will do't, for look you,
sir, he has as many friends as enemies; which friends,
sir, as it were, durst not – look you, sir – show themselves, as we term it, his friends whilst he's in directitude.

FIRST SERVINGMAN Directitude? What's that?

THIRD SERVINGMAN But when they shall see, sir, his
crest up again and the man in blood, they will out of their
burrows like conies after rain, and revel all with him.

FIRST SERVINGMAN But when goes this forward? 220

THIRD SERVINGMAN Tomorrow, today, presently. You
shall have the drum struck up this afternoon. 'Tis as it
were a parcel of their feast, and to be executed ere they
wipe their lips.

SECOND SERVINGMAN Why, then we shall have a stirring world again. This peace is nothing but to rust iron,
increase tailors, and breed ballad-makers.

FIRST SERVINGMAN Let me have war, say I. It exceeds
peace as far as day does night. It's sprightly walking,
audible, and full of vent. Peace is a very apoplexy, 230
lethargy; mulled, deaf, sleepy, insensible; a getter of
more bastard children than war's a destroyer of men.

SECOND SERVINGMAN 'Tis so. And as war in some sort
may be said to be a ravisher, so it cannot be denied but
peace is a great maker of cuckolds.

FIRST SERVINGMAN Ay, and it makes men hate one another.

THIRD SERVINGMAN Reason: because they then less need one another. The wars for my money. I hope to see
240  Romans as cheap as Volscians. They are rising, they are rising.

BOTH In, in, in, in.                                        *Exeunt*

*Tribunes in exultation — irony.*

IV.6            *Enter the two Tribunes, Sicinius and Brutus*

SICINIUS

We hear not of him, neither need we fear him. — *irony*
His remedies are tame – the present peace
And quietness of the people, which before
Were in wild hurry. Here do we make his friends
Blush that the world goes well, who rather had,
Though they themselves did suffer by't, behold
Dissentious numbers pestering streets than see
Our tradesmen singing in their shops and going
About their functions friendly. — *in friendship*

BRUTUS

10  We stood to't in good time.

              *Enter Menenius*

                              Is this Menenius?

SICINIUS

'Tis he, 'tis he. O, he is grown most kind
Of late. Hail, sir!

MENENIUS              Hail to you both!

SICINIUS

Your Coriolanus is not much missed
But with his friends. The commonwealth doth stand,
And so would do, were he more angry at it.

MENENIUS

All's well, and might have been much better if

156

He could have temporized. *) summary of Coriolanus*

SICINIUS                         Where is he, hear you?

MENENIUS

Nay, I hear nothing. His mother and his wife
Hear nothing from him.

  *Enter three or four Citizens*

CITIZENS

The gods preserve you both!

SICINIUS                         Good-e'en, our neighbours.   20

BRUTUS

Good-e'en to you all, good-e'en to you all.

FIRST CITIZEN

Ourselves, our wives and children, on our knees
Are bound to pray for you both.

SICINIUS                         Live and thrive!

BRUTUS

Farewell, kind neighbours. We wished Coriolanus
Had loved you as we did.

CITIZENS                         Now the gods keep you!

BOTH TRIBUNES

Farewell, farewell.     *Exeunt Citizens*

SICINIUS

This is a happier and more comely time
Than when these fellows ran about the streets
Crying confusion.

BRUTUS                         Caius Martius was
A worthy officer i'th'war, but insolent,   30
O'ercome with pride, ambitious past all thinking,
Self-loving –

SICINIUS         And affecting one sole throne *) he is rather*
Without assistance.   *associate*   *stupid to*

MENENIUS                         I think not so. *still believe*

SICINIUS   *this charge*

We should by this, to all our lamentation, *of*
          *Coriolanus*

157

If he had gone forth Consul, found it so.

BRUTUS

The gods have well prevented it, and Rome
Sits safe and still without him.

*Enter an Aedile*

AEDILE                                        Worthy Tribunes,
There is a slave, whom we have put in prison,
Reports the Volsces with two several powers
40 Are entered in the Roman territories,
And with the deepest malice of the war
Destroy what lies before 'em.

MENENIUS                              'Tis Aufidius,
Who, hearing of our Martius' banishment,
Thrusts forth his horns again into the world,
Which were inshelled when Martius stood for Rome,
And durst not once peep out.

SICINIUS

Come, what talk you of Martius?

BRUTUS

Go see this rumourer whipped. It cannot be
The Volsces dare break with us.

MENENIUS                              Cannot be!
50 We have record that very well it can,
And three examples of the like hath been
Within my age. But reason with the fellow
Before you punish him, where he heard this,
Lest you shall chance to whip your information
And beat the messenger who bids beware
Of what is to be dreaded.

SICINIUS                        Tell not me.
I know this cannot be.

BRUTUS                        Not possible.

*Enter a Messenger*

MESSENGER

The nobles in great earnestness are going

158

All to the Senate House. Some news is coming in
That turns their countenances.

SICINIUS                        'Tis this slave –                    60
Go whip him 'fore the people's eyes – his raising,
Nothing but his report.

MESSENGER                Yes, worthy sir,
The slave's report is seconded, and more,
More fearful is delivered.

SICINIUS                        What more fearful?

MESSENGER
It is spoke freely out of many mouths –
How probable I do not know – that Martius,
Joined with Aufidius, leads a power 'gainst Rome,
And vows revenge as spacious as between
The young'st and oldest thing.

SICINIUS                        This is most likely!

BRUTUS
Raised only that the weaker sort may wish            70
Good Martius home again.

SICINIUS                        The very trick on't.

MENENIUS
This is unlikely.
He and Aufidius can no more atone
Than violent'st contrariety.

                *Enter a second Messenger*

SECOND MESSENGER
You are sent for to the Senate.
A fearful army, led by Caius Martius
Associated with Aufidius, rages
Upon our territories, and have already
O'erborne their way, consumed with fire and took
What lay before them.                                80

                *Enter Cominius*

COMINIUS
O, you have made good work!

MENENIUS                              What news? What news?

COMINIUS

You have holp to ravish your own daughters and
To melt the city leads upon your pates,                    → lead-
To see your wives dishonoured to your noses –               covered
                                                            roofs

MENENIUS

What's the news? What's the news?

COMINIUS                          to their foundations

– Your temples burnèd in their cement, and
Your franchises, whereon you stood, confined               where
Into an auger's bore.                                       you were
                                                           stood-firr

MENENIUS                          Pray now, your news? –
You have made fair work, I fear me. – Pray, your news? –
90    If Martius should be joined wi'th'Volscians –

COMINIUS                                             If?

He is their god. He leads them like a thing
god –     Made by some other deity than Nature,
like      That shapes man better; and they follow him
qualities Against us brats with no less confidence
          Than boys pursuing summer butterflies,
          Or butchers killing flies.

MENENIUS                          You have made good work,
You and your apron-men, you that stood so much
Upon the voice of occupation and          men of
The breath of garlic-eaters!              handicraft

COMINIUS                          suggestion of low-
100    He'll shake your Rome about your ears.        class

MENENIUS

classical     As Hercules did shake down mellow fruit.
reference –   You have made fair work!
Hercules
BRUTUS
last
labour    But is this true, sir?

COMINIUS                          Ay, and you'll look pale
Before you find it other. All the regions

Do smilingly revolt, and who resists
Are mocked for valiant ignorance,
And perish constant fools. Who is't can blame him?
Your enemies and his find something in him.

MENENIUS

We are all undone unless
The noble man have mercy.

COMINIUS                    Who shall ask it?                110
The Tribunes cannot do't for shame; the people
Deserve such pity of him as the wolf
Does of the shepherds. For his best friends, if they
Should say 'Be good to Rome', they charged him even
As those should do that had deserved his hate,
And therein showed like enemies.

MENENIUS                                'Tis true.
If he were putting to my house the brand
That should consume it, I have not the face
To say 'Beseech you, cease.' You have made fair hands,
You and your crafts! You have crafted fair!

COMINIUS                            You have brought    120
A trembling upon Rome, such as was never
S'incapable of help.

TRIBUNES            Say not we brought it.

MENENIUS

How? Was't we? We loved him, but, like beasts
And cowardly nobles, gave way unto your clusters,
Who did hoot him out o'th'city.

COMINIUS                        But I fear
They'll roar him in again. Tullus Aufidius,
The second name of men, obeys his points
As if he were his officer. Desperation
Is all the policy, strength, and defence
That Rome can make against them.

        *Enter a troop of Citizens*

**MENENIUS** Here come the clusters.
And is Aufidius with him? You are they
That made the air unwholesome when you cast
Your stinking greasy caps in hooting
At Coriolanus' exile. Now he's coming,
And not a hair upon a soldier's head
Which will not prove a whip. As many coxcombs
As you threw caps up will he tumble down,
And pay you for your voices. 'Tis no matter.
If he could burn us all into one coal,
We have deserved it.

**CITIZENS**
Faith, we hear fearful news.

**FIRST CITIZEN** For mine own part,
When I said banish him, I said 'twas pity.

**SECOND CITIZEN** And so did I.

**THIRD CITIZEN** And so did I, and, to say the truth, so
did very many of us. That we did, we did for the best,
and though we willingly consented to his banishment,
yet it was against our will.

**COMINIUS**
Y'are goodly things, you voices!

**MENENIUS**
You have made good work,
You and your cry! Shall's to the Capitol?

**COMINIUS**
O, ay, what else? *Exeunt both*

**SICINIUS**
Go, masters, get you home. Be not dismayed;
These are a side that would be glad to have
This true which they so seem to fear. Go home,
And show no sign of fear.

**FIRST CITIZEN** The gods be good to us! Come, masters,
let's home. I ever said we were i'th'wrong when we
banished him.

SECOND CITIZEN So did we all. But come, let's home.

*Exeunt Citizens*

BRUTUS

I do not like this news.                                    160

SICINIUS

Nor I.

BRUTUS

Let's to the Capitol. Would half my wealth
Would buy this for a lie!

SICINIUS                    Pray let's go. *Exeunt Tribunes*


*Enter Aufidius, with his Lieutenant*                       IV.7

AUFIDIUS

Do they still fly to th'Roman?

LIEUTENANT

I do not know what witchcraft's in him, but
Your soldiers use him as the grace 'fore meat,
Their talk at table and their thanks at end,
And you are darkened in this action, sir,
Even by your own.

AUFIDIUS           I cannot help it now,
Unless by using means I lame the foot
Of our design. He bears himself more proudlier,
Even to my person, than I thought he would
When first I did embrace him. Yet his nature          10
In that's no changeling, and I must excuse
What cannot be amended.

LIEUTENANT              Yet I wish, sir –
I mean for your particular – you had not
Joined in commission with him, but either
Have borne the action of yourself, or else
To him had left it solely.

AUFIDIUS

I understand thee well, and be thou sure,

When he shall come to his account, he knows not
What I can urge against him. Although it seems,
20   And so he thinks, and is no less apparent
To th'vulgar eye, that he bears all things fairly
And shows good husbandry for the Volscian state,
Fights dragon-like, and does achieve as soon
As draw his sword; yet he hath left undone
That which shall break his neck or hazard mine
Whene'er we come to our account.

LIEUTENANT

Sir, I beseech you, think you he'll carry Rome?

AUFIDIUS

All places yield to him ere he sits down,
And the nobility of Rome are his.
30   The senators and patricians love him too.
The tribunes are no soldiers, and their people
Will be as rash in the repeal as hasty
To expel him thence. I think he'll be to Rome
As is the osprey to the fish, who takes it
By sovereignty of nature. First he was
A noble servant to them, but he could not
Carry his honours even. Whether 'twas pride,
Which out of daily fortune ever taints
The happy man; whether defect of judgement,
40   To fail in the disposing of those chances
Which he was lord of; or whether nature,
Not to be other than one thing, not moving
From th'casque to th'cushion, but commanding peace
Even with the same austerity and garb
As he controlled the war; but one of these –
As he hath spices of them all – not all,
For I dare so far free him – made him feared,
So hated, and so banished. But he has a merit
To choke it in the utterance. So our virtues

164

Lie in th'interpretation of the time; *[mercy]* *[any construction the 50]*
And power, unto itself most commendable, *[world chooses]*
Hath not a tomb so evident as a chair *[grave certain public] [rostrum] [to set]*
*[to praise]* *[upon them]*
T'extol what it hath done.
One fire drives out one fire; one nail one nail;
Rights by rights fuller, strengths by strengths do fail.
Come, let's away. When, Caius, Rome is thine,
Thou art poor'st of all; then shortly art thou mine.

*Exeunt*

*[See Coriolanus'* tragic failure to re-assert himself.]*

*Enter Menenius, Cominius, Sicinius and Brutus the* V.1
*two Tribunes, with others*

MENENIUS

No, I'll not go. You hear what he hath said *[Cominius]*
Which was sometime his general, who loved him
In a most dear particular. He called me father; *[warmth]*
But what o'that? Go, you that banished him,
A mile before his tent fall down, and knee
The way into his mercy. Nay, if he coyed
To hear Cominius speak, I'll keep at home. *[he nags]*

COMINIUS

He would not seem to know me.

MENENIUS                              Do you hear?

COMINIUS
*[to tribunes]*

Yet one time he did call me by my name.
I urged our old acquaintance and the drops                    10
That we have bled together. 'Coriolanus'
He would not answer to; forbade all names;
He was a kind of nothing, titleless,
Till he had forged himself a name i'th'fire
Of burning Rome.

*[Scenes 1 & 2 are build-ups to the big scene – Volumnia's mission on which rests the fate of a nation.]*

(pun on 2 combined works)
toiled with disastrous
acced

## V.1

MENENIUS                    Why, so! You have made good work.
A pair of Tribunes that have wracked for Rome
To make coals cheap – a noble memory!                    *memorial (ironic)*

COMINIUS
I minded him how royal 'twas to pardon
When it was less expected. He replied,
20      It was a bare petition of a state
To one whom they had punished.

MENENIUS
Very well. Could he say less?

COMINIUS
I offered to awaken his regard
For's private friends. His answer to me was,
He could not stay to pick them in a pile      *out from a pile of*
Of noisome musty chaff. He said 'twas folly,  *let the*
For one poor grain or two, to leave unburnt    *lot burn*
And still to nose th'offence.

MENENIUS
For one poor grain or two!
30      I am one of those; his mother, wife, his child,
And this brave fellow too – we are the grains.      *Cominius*
    *to tribunes* You are the musty chaff, and you are smelt
Above the moon. We must be burnt for you.

SICINIUS
Nay, pray be patient. If you refuse your aid
In this so-never-needed help, yet do not        *never*
Upbraid's with our distress. But sure, if you   *needed help*
Would be your country's pleader, your good tongue,  *so badly*
More than the instant army we can make,
Might stop our countryman.

MENENIUS                    No, I'll not meddle.

SICINIUS
40      Pray you go to him.

MENENIUS                    What should I do?

**BRUTUS**

    Only make trial what your love can do
    For Rome towards Martius.

**MENENIUS**               Well, and say that Martius

    Return me, as Cominius is returned,
    Unheard – what then?
    But as a discontented friend, grief-shot
    With his unkindness? Say't be so?

**SICINIUS**              Yet your good will

    Must have that thanks from Rome after the measure
    As you intended well.

**MENENIUS**        I'll undertake't;

    I think he'll hear me. Yet to bite his lip
    And hum at good Cominius much unhearts me.        50
    He was not taken well; he had not dined.
    The veins unfilled, our blood is cold, and then
    We pout upon the morning, are unapt
    To give or to forgive, but when we have stuffed
    These pipes and these conveyances of our blood
    With wine and feeding, we have suppler souls
    Than in our priest-like fasts. Therefore I'll watch him
    Till he be dieted to my request,
    And then I'll set upon him.

**BRUTUS**

    You know the very road into his kindness        60
    And cannot lose your way.

**MENENIUS**        Good faith, I'll prove him,

    Speed how it will. I shall ere long have knowledge
    Of my success.                        *Exit*

**COMINIUS**      He'll never hear him.

**SICINIUS**              Not?

**COMINIUS**

    I tell you he does sit in gold, his eye
    Red as 'twould burn Rome, and his injury

*pitiless*

(The gaoler to his pity.) I kneeled before him;
'Twas very faintly he said 'Rise', dismissed me
Thus with his speechless hand. What he would do
He sent in writing after me, what he would not,
70   Bound with an oath to yield to his conditions.
So that all hope is vain
Unless his noble mother and his wife,
Who, as I hear, mean to solicit him
For mercy to his country. Therefore let's hence,
And with our fair entreaties haste them on.    *Exeunt*

1st purpose? —pathos to contrast with next scene.

V.2      *Enter Menenius to the Watch on guard*

3rd purpose Coriolanus failure leading to = Volumnias attempt

FIRST WATCH
   Stay. Whence are you?

SECOND WATCH      Stand, and go back.

MENENIUS
   You guard like men, 'tis well. But, by your leave,
   I am an officer of state and come
   To speak with Coriolanus.

FIRST WATCH      From whence?

MENENIUS        From Rome.

FIRST WATCH
   You may not pass, you must return. Our general
   Will no more hear from thence.

2nd further weakening of Coriolanus's resolution

SECOND WATCH
   You'll see your Rome embraced with fire before
   You'll speak with Coriolanus.

MENENIUS      Good my friends,
   If you have heard your general talk of Rome
10   And of his friends there, it is lots to blanks  — 1,000 to 1 (odds on)
   My name hath touched your ears: it is Menenius.

FIRST WATCH
   Be it so; go back. The virtue of your name
   Is not here (passable.)  — pun — valid right to pass

MENENIUS                    I tell thee, fellow,
  Thy general is my lover. I have been
  The book of his good acts whence men have read
  His fame unparalleled haply amplified.
  For I have ever varnishèd my friends –
  Of whom he's chief – with all the size that verity
  Would without lapsing suffer. Nay, sometimes,
  Like to a bowl upon a subtle ground,
  I have tumbled past the throw, and in his praise
  Have almost stamped the leasing. Therefore, fellow,
  I must have leave to pass.

FIRST WATCH Faith, sir, if you had told as many lies in
  his behalf as you have uttered words in your own, you
  should not pass here; no, though it were as virtuous to
  lie as to live chastely. Therefore go back.

MENENIUS Prithee, fellow, remember my name is Menenius, always factionary on the party of your general.

SECOND WATCH Howsoever you have been his liar, as
  you say you have, I am one that, telling true under him,
  must say you cannot pass. Therefore go back.

MENENIUS Has he dined, canst thou tell? For I would not
  speak with him till after dinner.

FIRST WATCH You are a Roman, are you?

MENENIUS I am as thy general is.

FIRST WATCH Then you should hate Rome, as he does.
  Can you, when you have pushed out your gates the very
  defender of them, and in a violent popular ignorance
  given your enemy your shield, think to front his revenges
  with the easy groans of old women, the virginal palms of
  your daughters, or with the palsied intercession of such
  a decayed dotant as you seem to be? Can you think to
  blow out the intended fire your city is ready to flame in
  with such weak breath as this? No, you are deceived,
  therefore back to Rome and prepare for your execution.
  You are condemned, our general has sworn you out of

reprieve and pardon.

MENENIUS Sirrah, if thy captain knew I were here, he
50    would use me with estimation.

FIRST WATCH Come, my captain knows you not.

MENENIUS I mean thy general.

FIRST WATCH My general cares not for you. Back, I say,
go, lest I let forth your half-pint of blood. Back – that's
the utmost of your having. Back.

MENENIUS Nay, but fellow, fellow –

*Enter Coriolanus with Aufidius*

CORIOLANUS What's the matter?

MENENIUS Now, you companion, I'll say an errand for
you. You shall know now that I am in estimation. You
60    shall perceive that a Jack guardant cannot office me from
my son Coriolanus. Guess but my entertainment with
him. If thou stand'st not i'th'state of hanging, or of
some death more long in spectatorship and crueller in
suffering, behold now presently and swoon for what's to
come upon thee. (*To Coriolanus*) The glorious gods sit in
hourly synod about thy particular prosperity and love
thee no worse than thy old father Menenius does! O my
son, my son, thou art preparing fire for us. Look thee,
here's water to quench it. I was hardly moved to come
70    to thee; but being assured none but myself could move
thee, I have been blown out of your gates with sighs,
and conjure thee to pardon Rome and thy petitionary
countrymen. The good gods assuage thy wrath and turn
the dregs of it upon this varlet here – this, who, like a
block, hath denied my access to thee.

CORIOLANUS Away!

MENENIUS How? Away?

CORIOLANUS
Wife, mother, child, I know not. My affairs
Are servanted to others. Though I owe

170

My revenue properly, my remission lies     80
In Volscian breasts. That we have been familiar,
Ingrate forgetfulness shall poison rather
Than pity note how much. Therefore be gone.
Mine ears against your suits are stronger than
Your gates against my force. Yet, for I loved thee,
Take this along. I writ it for thy sake (*gives a letter*)
And would have sent it. Another word, Menenius,
I will not hear thee speak. This man, Aufidius,
Was my beloved in Rome; yet thou behold'st.

AUFIDIUS

You keep a constant temper.     *Exeunt* 90

   *The Guard and Menenius stay behind*

FIRST WATCH Now, sir, is your name Menenius?

SECOND WATCH 'Tis a spell, you see, of much power.
You know the way home again.

FIRST WATCH Do you hear how we are shent for keeping
your greatness back?

SECOND WATCH What cause do you think I have to
swoon?

MENENIUS I neither care for th'world nor your general.
For such things as you, I can scarce think there's any,
y'are so slight. He that hath a will to die by himself fears   100
it not from another. Let your general do his worst. For
you, be that you are, long; and your misery increase
with your age! I say to you, as I was said to, Away!

    *Exit*

FIRST WATCH A noble fellow, I warrant him.

SECOND WATCH The worthy fellow is our general. He's
the rock, the oak not to be wind-shaken.   *Exit Watch*

*Handwritten at top: Climax of the play. Coriolanus & his mother clash — determine Coriolanus 2nd failure:*

V.3                    *Enter Coriolanus and Aufidius with others. They sit*

CORIOLANUS

We will before the walls of Rome tomorrow
Set down our host. My partner in this action,
You must report to th'Volscian lords how plainly *openly*
I have borne this business.

AUFIDIUS                         Only their ends
You have respected; stopped your ears against
The general suit of Rome; never admitted
A private whisper – no, not with such friends
That thought them sure of you.

CORIOLANUS                              This last old man,
Whom with a cracked heart I have sent to Rome,

10       Loved me above the measure of a father,
Nay, godded me indeed. Their latest refuge *last resort*
*god – like suggestion*  Was to send him; for whose old love I have –
Though I showed sourly to him – once more offered
The first conditions, which they did refuse
And cannot now accept, to grace him only
That thought he could do more. A very little
I have yielded to. Fresh embassies and suits,
Nor from the state nor private friends, hereafter
Will I lend ear to. (*Shouts within*) Ha! What shout is
this?

20       (*aside*) Shall I be tempted to infringe my vow
In the same time 'tis made? I will not.
            *Enter Virgilia, Volumnia, Valeria, young Martius,*
            *with Attendants*
My wife comes foremost, then the honoured mould
Wherein this trunk was framed, and in her hand
The grandchild to her blood. But out, affection!
*family ties*  All bond and privilege of nature, break!
Let it be virtuous to be obstinate. — *unyielding*
What is that curtsy worth? Or those dove's eyes

172

Which can make gods forsworn? I melt, and am not
Of stronger earth than others. My mother bows,
As if Olympus to a molehill should                                    30
In supplication nod, and my young boy
Hath an aspect of intercession which      → pleading look
Great Nature cries 'Deny not.' Let the Volsces
Plough Rome and harrow Italy! I'll never
Be such a gosling to obey instinct, but stand
As if a man were author of himself
And knew no other kin.

VIRGILIA                    My lord and husband!

CORIOLANUS
These eyes are not the same I wore in Rome.    → sees things differently

VIRGILIA
The sorrow that delivers us thus changed
Makes you think so.

CORIOLANUS (*aside*)  Like a dull actor now                          40
I have forgot my part and I am out,    → stage term — actor forgetting his lines
Even to a full disgrace. (*Rising and going to her*) Best of
    my flesh,
Forgive my tyranny; but do not say
For that, 'Forgive our Romans.' O, a kiss
Long as my exile, sweet as my revenge!
Now, by the jealous queen of heaven, that kiss    → reference to Juno — goddess of marriage
I carried from thee, dear, and my true lip
Hath virgined it e'er since. You gods! I pray,
And the most noble mother of the world
Leave unsaluted. Sink my knee i'th'earth;                            50
    *He kneels*
Of thy deep duty more impression show
Than that of common sons.

VOLUMNIA                    O, stand up blest!    irony ?
    *He rises*
Whilst with no softer cushion than the flint

173

I kneel before thee, and unproperly
Show duty as mistaken all this while
Between the child and parent.

*She kneels*

CORIOLANUS                     What's this?
Your knees to me? To your corrected son?

*He raises her*

Then let the pebbles on the hungry beach
Fillip the stars. Then let the mutinous winds
60  Strike the proud cedars 'gainst the fiery sun,
Murdering impossibility, to make
What cannot be slight work.

VOLUMNIA                     Thou art my warrior;
I holp to frame thee. Do you know this lady?

CORIOLANUS
The noble sister of Publicola,
The moon of Rome, chaste as the icicle
That's curdied by the frost from purest snow
And hangs on Dian's temple – dear Valeria!

VOLUMNIA (*indicating young Martius*)
This is a poor epitome of yours,
Which by th'interpretation of full time
70  May show like all yourself.

CORIOLANUS                     The god of soldiers,
With the consent of supreme Jove, inform
Thy thoughts with nobleness, that thou mayst prove
To shame unvulnerable, and stick i'th'wars
Like a great sea-mark, standing every flaw
And saving those that eye thee!

VOLUMNIA                     Your knee, sirrah.

CORIOLANUS
That's my brave boy!

VOLUMNIA
Even he, your wife, this lady, and myself

174

Are suitors to you.

CORIOLANUS    I beseech you, peace!
Or, if you'd ask, remember this before:
The thing I have forsworn to grant may never            80
Be held by you denials. Do not bid me
Dismiss my soldiers, or capitulate ⟩ — discuss terms
Again with Rome's mechanics. Tell me not → contemptuous
Wherein I seem unnatural. Desire not                  term for
T'allay my rages and revenges with              the craftsmen
Your colder reasons.                                  of Rome

VOLUMNIA    O, no more, no more!
You have said you will not grant us any thing –
For we have nothing else to ask but that
Which you deny already. Yet we will ask,
That, if you fail in our request, the blame  → to grant   90
May hang upon your hardness. Therefore hear us.    it

CORIOLANUS

Aufidius, and you Volsces, mark; for we'll
Hear naught from Rome in private. (*He sits*) Your
        request?

VOLUMNIA

Should we be silent and not speak, our raiment
And state of bodies would bewray what life
We have led since thy exile. Think with thyself
How more unfortunate than all living women
Are we come hither; since that thy sight, which should
Make our eyes flow with joy, hearts dance with comforts,
Constrains them weep and shake with fear and sorrow,  100
Making the mother, wife, and child to see
The son, the husband, and the father tearing
His country's bowels out. And to poor we
Thine enmity's most capital. Thou barr'st us
Our prayers to the gods, which is a comfort
That all but we enjoy. For how can we,

V.3

Alas, how can we for our country pray,
Whereto we are bound, together with thy victory,
Whereto we are bound? Alack, or we must lose
The country, our dear nurse, or else thy person,
Our comfort in the country. We must find
An evident calamity, though we had
Our wish, which side should win. For either thou
Must as a foreign recreant be led
With manacles through our streets, or else
Triumphantly tread on thy country's ruin,
And bear the palm for having bravely shed
Thy wife and children's blood. For myself, son,
I purpose not to wait on fortune till
These wars determine. If I cannot persuade thee
Rather to show a noble grace to both parts
Than seek the end of one, thou shalt no sooner
March to assault thy country than to tread –
Trust to't, thou shalt not – on thy mother's womb
That brought thee to this world.

VIRGILIA                                    Ay, and mine,
That brought you forth this boy to keep your name
Living to time.

BOY                         'A shall not tread on me!
I'll run away till I am bigger, but then I'll fight.

CORIOLANUS

Not of a woman's tenderness to be
Requires nor child nor woman's face to see.
I have sat too long.

          *He rises*

VOLUMNIA                    Nay, go not from us thus.
If it were so that our request did tend
To save the Romans, thereby to destroy
The Volsces whom you serve, you might condemn us
As poisonous of your honour. No, our suit

176

Is that you reconcile them, while the Volsces
May say 'This mercy we have showed', the Romans
'This we received', and each in either side
Give the all-hail to thee and cry 'Be blest
For making up this peace!' Thou know'st, great son,                    140
The end of war's uncertain; but this certain,
That, if thou conquer Rome, the benefit
Which thou shalt thereby reap is such a name
Whose repetition will be dogged with curses,
Whose chronicle thus writ: 'The man was noble,
But with his last attempt he wiped it out,
Destroyed his country, and his name remains
To th'ensuing age abhorred.' Speak to me, son.
Thou hast affected the fine strains of honour,
To imitate the graces of the gods,                                     150
To tear with thunder the wide cheeks o'th'air,
And yet to charge thy sulphur with a bolt
That should but rive an oak. Why dost not speak?
Think'st thou it honourable for a nobleman
Still to remember wrongs? Daughter, speak you:
He cares not for your weeping. Speak thou, boy.
Perhaps thy childishness will move him more
Than can our reasons. There's no man in the world
More bound to's mother, yet here he lets me prate
Like one i'th'stocks. Thou hast never in thy life                       160
Showed thy dear mother any courtesy,
When she, poor hen, fond of no second brood,
Has clucked thee to the wars, and safely home
Loaden with honour. Say my request's unjust,
And spurn me back. But if it be not so,
Thou art not honest, and the gods will plague thee
That thou restrain'st from me the duty which
To a mother's part belongs. He turns away.
Down ladies! Let us shame him with our knees.

170   To his surname Coriolanus 'longs more pride
Than pity to our prayers. Down! An end;
    *The four kneel*
This is the last. So, we will home to Rome,
And die among our neighbours. Nay, behold's!
This boy, that cannot tell what he would have
But kneels and holds up hands for fellowship,
Does reason our petition with more strength
Than thou hast to deny't. Come, let us go.
    *They rise*
This fellow had a Volscian to his mother;
His wife is in Corioles, and his child
180   Like him by chance. Yet give us our dispatch.
I am hushed until our city be afire,
And then I'll speak a little.

CORIOLANUS
    *Holds her by the hand, silent*
O, mother, mother!
What have you done? Behold, the heavens do ope,
The gods look down, and this unnatural scene
They laugh at. O my mother, mother! O!
You have won a happy victory to Rome.
But for your son – believe it, O believe it –
Most dangerously you have with him prevailed,
190   If not most mortal to him. But let it come.
Aufidius, though I cannot make true wars,
I'll frame convenient peace. Now, good Aufidius,
Were you in my stead, would you have heard
A mother less? Or granted less, Aufidius?

AUFIDIUS
I was moved withal.

CORIOLANUS      I dare be sworn you were!
And, sir, it is no little thing to make
Mine eyes to sweat compassion. But, good sir,

What peace you'll make, advise me. For my part,
I'll not to Rome, I'll back with you, and pray you
Stand to me in this cause. O mother! Wife!          200

AUFIDIUS (*aside*)
I am glad thou hast set thy mercy and thy honour
At difference in thee. Out of that I'll work
Myself a former fortune.

CORIOLANUS (*to the ladies*) Ay, by and by.
But we will drink together; and you shall bear
A better witness back than words, which we,
On like conditions, will have counter-sealed.
Come, enter with us. Ladies, you deserve
To have a temple built you. All the swords
In Italy, and her confederate arms,
Could not have made this peace.          *Exeunt* 210

*Enter Menenius and Sicinius*          V.4

MENENIUS See you yond coign o'th'Capitol, yond corner-
stone?

SICINIUS Why, what of that?

MENENIUS If it be possible for you to displace it with
your little finger, there is some hope the ladies of Rome,
especially his mother, may prevail with him. But I say
there is no hope in't, our throats are sentenced and stay
upon execution.

SICINIUS Is't possible that so short a time can alter the
condition of a man?          10

MENENIUS There is difference between a grub and a
butterfly, yet your butterfly was a grub. This Martius is
grown from man to dragon. He has wings, he's more
than a creeping thing.

SICINIUS He loved his mother dearly.

MENENIUS So did he me; and he no more remembers his
mother now than an eight-year-old horse. The tartness

179

of his face sours ripe grapes. When he walks, he moves
like an engine, and the ground shrinks before his tread-
20 ing. He is able to pierce a corslet with his eye, talks like
a knell, and his hum is a battery. He sits in his state as a
thing made for Alexander. What he bids be done is
finished with his bidding. He wants nothing of a god but
eternity and a heaven to throne in.

SICINIUS Yes, mercy, if you report him truly.

MENENIUS I paint him in the character. Mark what mercy
his mother shall bring from him. There is no more
mercy in him than there is milk in a male tiger. That
shall our poor city find. And all this is 'long of you.

30 SICINIUS The gods be good unto us!

MENENIUS No, in such a case the gods will not be good
unto us. When we banished him we respected not them;
and, he returning to break our necks, they respect not us.

*Enter a Messenger*

MESSENGER

Sir, if you'd save your life, fly to your house.
The plebeians have got your fellow Tribune
And hale him up and down, all swearing if
The Roman ladies bring not comfort home
They'll give him death by inches.

*Enter another Messenger*

SICINIUS                              What's the news?

SECOND MESSENGER

Good news, good news! The ladies have prevailed,
40 The Volscians are dislodged and Martius gone.
A merrier day did never yet greet Rome,
No, not th'expulsion of the Tarquins.

SICINIUS                              Friend,
Art thou certain this is true? Is't most certain?

SECOND MESSENGER

As certain as I know the sun is fire.

Where have you lurked that you make doubt of it?
Ne'er through an arch so hurried the blown tide
As the recomforted through th'gates. Why, hark you!

    *Trumpets, hautboys, drums beat, all together*

The trumpets, sackbuts, psalteries, and fifes,
Tabors and cymbals and the shouting Romans
Make the sun dance. Hark you!

    *A shout within*

MENENIUS                  This is good news.    50
  I will go meet the ladies. This Volumnia
  Is worth of consuls, senators, patricians,
  A city full; of tribunes such as you,
  A sea and land full. You have prayed well today.
  This morning for ten thousand of your throats
  I'd not have given a doit. Hark, how they joy!

    *Sound still with the shouts*

SICINIUS
  First, the gods bless you for your tidings; next,
  Accept my thankfulness.

SECOND MESSENGER
  Sir, we have all great cause to give great thanks.

SICINIUS
  They are near the city?                    60

SECOND MESSENGER
  Almost at point to enter.

SICINIUS
  We'll meet them, and help the joy.    *Exeunt*


    *Enter two Senators, with Volumnia, Virgilia, and* V.5
    *Valeria, passing over the stage, with other Lords*

FIRST SENATOR
  Behold our patroness, the life of Rome!
  Call all your tribes together, praise the gods,

And make triumphant fires; strew flowers before them.
Unshout the noise that banished Martius,
Repeal him with the welcome of his mother.
Cry 'Welcome, ladies, welcome!'

ALL

Welcome, ladies, welcome!

*A flourish with drums and trumpets. Exeunt*

V.6                    *Enter Tullus Aufidius, with Attendants*

AUFIDIUS

Go tell the lords o'th'city I am here.
Deliver them this paper. Having read it,
Bid them repair to th'market-place, where I,
Even in theirs and in the commons' ears,
Will vouch the truth of it. Him I accuse
The city ports by this hath entered and
Intends t'appear before the people, hoping
To purge himself with words. Dispatch.

*Exeunt Attendants*
*Enter three or four Conspirators of Aufidius's faction*

Most welcome!

FIRST CONSPIRATOR

10   How is it with our general?

AUFIDIUS                    Even so
As with a man by his own alms empoisoned
And with his charity slain.

SECOND CONSPIRATOR        Most noble sir,
If you do hold the same intent wherein
You wished us parties, we'll deliver you
Of your great danger.

AUFIDIUS              Sir, I cannot tell.
We must proceed as we do find the people.

THIRD CONSPIRATOR

The people will remain uncertain whilst

182

V.6

'Twixt you there's difference. But the fall of either
Makes the survivor heir of all.

AUFIDIUS                                I know it,
And my pretext to strike at him admits                        20
A good construction. I raised him, and I pawned
Mine honour for his truth; who being so heightened,
He watered his new plants with dews of flattery,
Seducing so my friends. And to this end
He bowed his nature, never known before
But to be rough, unswayable and free.

THIRD CONSPIRATOR
Sir, his stoutness
When he did stand for consul, which he lost
By lack of stooping –

AUFIDIUS                      That I would have spoke of.
Being banished for't, he came unto my hearth,        30
Presented to my knife his throat. I took him,
Made him joint-servant with me, gave him way
In all his own desires; nay, let him choose
Out of my files, his projects to accomplish,
My best and freshest men; served his designments
In mine own person; holp to reap the fame
Which he did end all his, and took some pride
To do myself this wrong. Till at the last
I seemed his follower, not partner; and
He waged me with his countenance as if        40
I had been mercenary.

FIRST CONSPIRATOR    So he did, my lord;
The army marvelled at it. And, in the last,
When we had carried Rome and that we looked
For no less spoil than glory –

AUFIDIUS                      There was it,
For which my sinews shall be stretched upon him.
At a few drops of women's rheum, which are

183

As cheap as lies, he sold the blood and labour
Of our great action. Therefore shall he die,
And I'll renew me in his fall. But hark!
*Drums and trumpets sound, with great shouts of the
people*

FIRST CONSPIRATOR
50     Your native town you entered like a post, *mere messenger*
And had no welcomes home; but he returns
Splitting the air with noise.

SECOND CONSPIRATOR     And patient fools,
Whose children he hath slain, their base throats tear
With giving him glory.

THIRD CONSPIRATOR    Therefore, at your vantage,
Ere he express himself or move the people
With what he would say, let him feel your sword,
Which we will second. When he lies along, *stretched out dead*
*version?* After your way his tale pronounced shall bury
His reasons with his body.

AUFIDIUS             Say no more.
60     Here come the Lords.
*Enter the Lords of the city*

ALL LORDS
You are most welcome home.

AUFIDIUS         I have not deserved it.
But, worthy Lords, have you with heed perused
What I have written to you?

ALL         We have.

FIRST LORD    *committed*      And grieve to hear't.
What faults he made before the last, I think
Might have found easy fines. But there to end
Where he was to begin, and give away
The benefit of our levies, answering us
With our own charge, making a treaty where

184

There was a yielding – this admits no excuse.
AUFIDIUS
He approaches. You shall hear him.                          70
   *Enter Coriolanus, marching with drum and colours;*
   *the Commoners being with him*
CORIOLANUS
Hail, Lords! I am returned your soldier,
No more infected with my country's love
Than when I parted hence, but still subsisting
Under your great command. You are to know
That prosperously I have attempted and
With bloody passage led your wars even to
The gates of Rome. Our spoils we have brought home
Doth more than counterpoise a full third part
The charges of the action. We have made peace
With no less honour to the Antiates            80
Than shame to th'Romans. And we here deliver,
Subscribed by th'consuls and patricians,
Together with the seal o'th'Senate, what
We have compounded on.
AUFIDIUS                    Read it not, noble Lords;
But tell the traitor in the highest degree
He hath abused your powers.
CORIOLANUS
Traitor? How now?
AUFIDIUS                    Ay, traitor, Martius!
CORIOLANUS                                        Martius?
AUFIDIUS
Ay, Martius, Caius Martius! Dost thou think
I'll grace thee with that robbery, thy stolen name
Coriolanus in Corioles?                          90
You lords and heads o'th'state, perfidiously
He has betrayed your business and given up,
For certain drops of salt, your city Rome –

I say your city – to his wife and mother,
Breaking his oath and resolution like
A twist of rotten silk, never admitting
Counsel o'th'war. But at his nurse's tears
He whined and roared away your victory,
That pages blushed at him and men of heart
100   Looked wondering each at others.

CORIOLANUS                Hear'st thou, Mars?

AUFIDIUS
Name not the god, thou boy of tears!

CORIOLANUS             Ha?

AUFIDIUS
No more.

CORIOLANUS
Measureless liar, thou hast made my heart
Too great for what contains it. 'Boy'! O slave!
Pardon me, Lords, 'tis the first time that ever
I was forced to scold. Your judgements, my grave Lords,
Must give this cur the lie; and his own notion –
Who wears my stripes impressed upon him, that
Must bear my beating to his grave – shall join
110   To thrust the lie unto him.

FIRST LORD
Peace, both, and hear me speak.

CORIOLANUS
Cut me to pieces, Volsces. Men and lads,
Stain all your edges on me. 'Boy'! False hound!
If you have writ your annals true, 'tis there
That, like an eagle in a dove-cote, I
Fluttered your Volscians in Corioles.
Alone I did it. 'Boy'!

AUFIDIUS            Why, noble Lords,
Will you be put in mind of his blind fortune,
Which was your shame, by this unholy braggart,

'Fore your own eyes and ears?

ALL CONSPIRATORS            Let him die for't.

ALL THE PEOPLE Tear him to pieces! – Do it presently!
– He killed my son! – My daughter! – He killed my
cousin Marcus! – He killed my father!

SECOND LORD

Peace, ho! No outrage. Peace!
The man is noble and his fame folds in
This orb o'th'earth. His last offences to us
Shall have judicious hearing. Stand, Aufidius,
And trouble not the peace.

CORIOLANUS            O that I had him,
With six Aufidiuses or more – his tribe,
To use my lawful sword!

AUFIDIUS            Insolent villain!         130

ALL CONSPIRATORS

Kill, kill, kill, kill, kill him!

> *The Conspirators draw their swords, and kill Martius,*
> *who falls*
> *Aufidius stands on him*

LORDS

Hold, hold, hold, hold!

AUFIDIUS

My noble masters, hear me speak.

FIRST LORD            O Tullus!

SECOND LORD

Thou hast done a deed whereat valour will weep.

THIRD LORD

Tread not upon him. Masters all, be quiet.
Put up your swords.

AUFIDIUS

My Lords, when you shall know – as in this rage
Provoked by him you cannot – the great danger
Which this man's life did owe you, you'll rejoice

140     That he is thus cut off. Please it your honours
To call me to your Senate, I'll deliver
Myself your loyal servant, or endure
Your heaviest censure.

FIRST LORD           Bear from hence his body,
And mourn you for him. Let him be regarded
As the most noble corse that ever herald
Did follow to his urn.

SECOND LORD         His own impatience
Takes from Aufidius a great part of blame.
Let's make the best of it.

AUFIDIUS            My rage is gone,
And I am struck with sorrow. Take him up.
150     Help three o'th'chiefest soldiers; I'll be one.
Beat thou the drum, that it speak mournfully.
Trail your steel pikes. Though in this city he
Hath widowed and unchilded many a one,
Which to this hour bewail the injury,
Yet he shall have a noble memory.
Assist.

*Exeunt, bearing the body of Martius.*
*A dead march sounded*

# COMMENTARY

THE Act and scene divisions are those of Peter Alexander's edition of the *Complete Works*, London, 1951. All references to other plays by Shakespeare, not yet published in the New Penguin Shakespeare, are to Alexander.

I.1    In this scene, which not only provides the play with a bustling and arresting opening (a great advantage in a theatre where there were no lights to go down) but also establishes the central conflict out of which the rest of the action grows, Shakespeare skilfully combines two separate incidents in Plutarch's narrative into one. The first (*Shakespeare's Plutarch*, pp. 300–305) was a rebellion of the people against 'the sore oppression of usurers'. This was pacified by the diplomacy of Menenius and by the concession to the people of the right to choose five tribunes annually to defend them from 'violence and oppression'. The second uprising, which occurred shortly before the time when Coriolanus stood for the consulship, was the result of a famine in Rome (pp. 314–24). On both occasions the people expressed their dissatisfaction by refusing to do military service.

(stage direction) *mutinous* rebellious, riotous

7    *Caius Martius*. The correct form of the hero's name in Latin is 'Caius Marcius'. 'Martius' is preferred in this edition, contrary to the practice of most editors, for three reasons: it is consistently so given in the Folio; it was the form Shakespeare found in North and in Holland's translation of Livy; it indicates, and may even have influenced, Shakespeare's view of Coriolanus's character. He is a 'son of Mars'.

11    *verdict* unanimous decision

189

15    *good* rich, substantial

       *authority* (the patricians, the ruling class)

17    *wholesome* good, fit to eat

       *guess* think, deduce

18    *humanely* out of fellow-feeling

18–21    *But they think we are too dear . . . them.* The general
       sense of this passage, which states the exact opposite of
       all that is conveyed by the word 'humanely' is: 'They
       prefer to keep us as we are, because the sight of our
       wretchedness makes them realize with pleasure pre-
       cisely how well off they are.'

18    *dear* precious, valuable

19    *object* spectacle

       *inventory* detailed list, set of meagre figures (like the
       citizens) representing large possessions

20    *particularize* give details of

       *sufferance* distress, suffering

22    *rakes.* 'As lean as a rake' is proverbial. Later in the scene
       Martius jeers at the citizens' addiction to proverbs.

26    *a very dog* a merciless enemy

35    *famously* gloriously, in a way that made him renowned

       *to that end* with that purpose (the winning of personal
       fame) in mind

       *soft-conscienced* easy-going, with no real convictions

37    *to be partly proud* partly to be proud

38    *even to the altitude of his virtue.* The First Citizen means
       that Martius's pride is as excessive as his valour.

44    (stage direction) *Shouts within.* Shakespeare, characteris-
       tically, is thinking in terms of his stage. *Within* means
       'in the tiring-house, off stage'.

45    *o'th'* of the (colloquial)

46    *To th'* to the (colloquial)

       *Capitol* citadel of Rome

48    *Soft* stay, wait a moment

49    *Worthy Menenius Agrippa.* It was Plutarch who supplied
       Shakespeare with the groundwork for this character and
       suggested his affable manner with the citizens. He

writes: 'The Senate . . . did send unto them certain of the pleasantest old men and the most acceptable to the people among them. Of those Menenius Agrippa was he who was sent for chief man. . . .' As befits his rank, Menenius speaks blank verse, but his language is colloquial and friendly.

54  *bats* cudgels (the weapons of the London apprentices)

55  FIRST CITIZEN. The Folio assigns this speech and the rest of the dialogue with Menenius to the Second Citizen. This must be wrong, since the Second Citizen is kindly disposed towards Menenius and Martius. It is the First Citizen who is the leader of the crowd and its mouthpiece.

61  *undo* ruin

64  *For* as for

67  *on* continue on

68  *curbs.* A curb is a chain attached to the part of a bridle known as the bit, and is used to check an unruly horse. Here it is employed figuratively to mean restraints or hindrances.

70  *your impediment* the obstruction you create

73  *transported* carried away

74  *attends* awaits

75  *helms* helmsmen, pilots

81  *piercing* oppressive, severe

90  *stale't* make it stale

92  *fob off* dispose of, or get rid of, by a trick
    *disgrace* misfortune, calamity
    *an't* if it (colloquial)

96  *gulf* bottomless pit, whirlpool

97  *I'th* in the (colloquial)

98  *Still* always, continually

99  *where* whereas
    *instruments* organs

100  *devise* ponder, deliberate

101  *participate* participating

102  *affection* inclination, wish

105–6     *a kind of smile, | Which ne'er came from the lungs* a super-
cilious smile, as distinct from a belly-laugh – Menenius
makes the belly very much a patrician.

108     *tauntingly.* The Folio reads 'taintingly' which has been
explained as 'so as to put to shame', but *tauntingly* fits
the manner in which the belly eventually gives its
answer.

110     *envied his receipt* envied it for what it received
*fitly* justly (used ironically)

112–22     *Your belly's answer . . . belly answer?* The reversal of roles
here, with the First Citizen taking up the allegory and
Menenius asking the questions, is a fine example of
Shakespeare's skill in breaking up a piece of narrative
to give it dramatic life.

113–17     *The kingly crownèd head . . . our fabric.* The analogy between the state and the human body was one of the
great commonplaces of Shakespeare's time (see Introduction, p. 24). The head, as the seat of reason, was
king of the little state of man; and the heart, as the seat
of understanding, was the place of counsel and deliberation.

116     *muniments* supports

118     *'Fore me* upon my word

119     *cormorant* greedy, insatiable (frequently applied to
usurers in Shakespeare's day)

120     *sink* cesspool

124     *you'st* you'll (provincial)

125     *Y'are* ye are (colloquial)

128     *incorporate* united in one body

131     *shop* workshop

134     *to the court, the heart, to th'seat o'th'brain* to the court
or place of counsel (that is, the heart) and thence to the
throne itself (that is, the brain)

135     *cranks* winding passages
*offices* inferior rooms

136     *nerves* sinews, muscles

143     *flour.* In the Folio this word is 'Flowre'. It is clearly

intended to carry the sense of 'fine essence' in addition
to its literal meaning.

144   *to't* to it (colloquial)

148   *digest* understand, interpret (with a play on the normal
      sense)

149   *weal o'th'common* welfare of the state

157–8  *Thou rascal, that art worst in blood to run, | Lead'st first
      to win some vantage.* A rascal was a deer in poor condi-
      tion ('worst in blood'), but the word could also be used
      of a dog, which fits this context better. Dr Johnson para-
      phrases thus: 'Thou that art a hound, or running dog
      of the lowest breed, lead'st the pack, when anything is
      to be gotten.'

161   *have bale* get the worst of it, be destroyed

162   *Thanks.* This entry is a telling one. Dismissing com-
      pliments with a single word, Martius rounds on the
      citizens.

164   *scabs.* This word has two meanings, both of which are
      relevant: (1) scabs raised by scratching oneself; (2)
      scurvy rogues. Martius regards the people's grievances
      as superficial and self-inflicted.

167   *nor peace* neither peace

168   *proud* high-spirited (and, therefore, ungovernable)

171   *the coal of fire upon the ice.* This image is probably an
      allusion to the Great Frost of 1607–8, when the Thames
      was frozen over and 'pans of coals' were placed on the
      ice to enable people to warm their hands.

172–4  *Your virtue is | To make him worthy whose offence sub-
      dues him | And curse that justice did it* your peculiar
      quality is to make a hero of the man whose offence
      subjects him to the law, and to curse the justice that
      punishes him

182   *garland* pride, chief ornament

186   *seeking* suit, petition

191   *side* take sides with

193   *feebling* depreciating, making weak

195   *ruth* pity

196    *quarry* heap of slaughtered deer

197    *quartered* cut into four pieces (the punishment inflicted on traitors in Shakespeare's day)

198    *pick* pitch, hurl

199    *almost.* Some editors emend to 'all most'.

201    *passing* extremely, exceedingly

209    *To break the heart of generosity* to give the final blow to the nobility – Latin *generosus*, of good birth

212    *Shouting their emulation* rivalling each other in shouting

215    *'Sdeath* God's death (an oath)

218    *Win upon power* take advantage of the power already won to win more

218–19    *themes | For insurrection's arguing* subjects for rebels to discuss

223    *on't* of it
       *vent* get rid of

227    *to't* to the test

230    *together* against each other. The Folio reads 'together?', but it is inconceivable that Cominius should not know of the long-standing rivalry between Martius and Aufidius.

232    *party* side

237    *I am constant* I keep my word

239    *Stand'st out?* Do you refuse to take part?

245    *Right worthy you priority* you fully deserve pride of place

249    *puts well forth* blossoms, makes a fine show
       (stage direction) *stay behind*. The Folio reads: '*Manent.*'

254    *moved* moved to anger, exasperated
       *spare to gird* refrain from mocking at

256–7    *The present wars devour him; he is grown | Too proud to be so valiant* the present wars eat him up with increased pride in his own valour. Many editors read 'The present wars devour him!' – that is, 'May the coming wars eat him up!'

258    *Tickled* flattered, gratified
       *success* fortune, result

260–61    *to be commanded* | *Under* to be under the command of

261–2    *Fame, at the which he aims . . . graced.* Fame is thought of at first as an object to be aimed at, hence the use of 'which'; then as a goddess whose favours Martius has received, hence the use of 'whom'.

269    *Opinion* (1) honour, reputation; (2) public opinion
       *sticks* is set

270    *demerits* deserts, merits

275    *dispatch* final arrangements

276    *More than his singularity* with an even greater display of pride and self-importance than usual


I.2    Plutarch does not mention Aufidius until after the banishment of Coriolanus (*Shakespeare's Plutarch*, p. 334) though he does say then that they 'had encountered many times together'. Shakespeare, with the dramatist's feeling for conflict, introduces the rivalry between them into his first scene and brings on Aufidius himself in the second.

2    *entered in* acquainted with, in the secret of

4    *What* what things, what plans

6    *circumvention* knowledge to circumvent it

9    *pressed a power* levied an army

20    *pretences* plans, designs

22    *appeared* became apparent
       *discovery* disclosure

24    *take in* capture
       *almost* even

27    *Let us alone* trust us

28    *set down before's* besiege us
       *for the remove* to raise the siege

32    *parcels* parts, portions


I.3    This quiet domestic scene, which is of Shakespeare's own invention, is in marked contrast to the public scenes preceding it. Through it he conveys much about

Coriolanus's upbringing and his relationship with his mother, which is vital for the further development of the action. The *two low stools* would indicate to his audience that the scene is set indoors.

2      *comfortable sort* cheerful manner

10     *such a person* such a fine figure of a man
       *it* this fine figure

11     *hang by th'wall* be a mere ornament
       *made it not stir* did not give it movement

13     *a cruel war* (the war against the Tarquins, in which Coriolanus saved the life of a fellow-soldier and was 'crowned with a garland of oaken boughs' for doing so)

18     *But had he died.* Virgilia's first words indicate her nature; she is concerned for life.

25     *surfeit* spend his time in self-indulgence

34     *Come on, you cowards!* These words look forward to the next scene and prepare the way for it. They also show whence the hero derives his attitude towards his fellow-soldiers.
       *got* begotten

37     *tasked* employed, set a task

37–8   *to mow | Or all or lose his hire* either to mow the whole (of the field) or to lose his wages

41     *trophy* monument
       *Hecuba* (wife of Priam, king of Troy, and mother of Hector, the Trojan champion)

44     *At Grecian sword, contemning. Tell Valeria.* The Folio reads: 'At Grecian sword. *Contenning*, tell *Valeria*' – the compositor having apparently taken 'Contenning' to be the name of the gentlewoman.

46     *bless* guard, protect

47–8   *He'll beat Aufidius' head below his knee . . . neck.* This proud boast is a piece of unconscious irony.

48     (stage direction) *Usher* a male attendant on a lady

52     *How do you both?* how are you both?
       *You are manifest housekeepers* you have clearly settled down to a day indoors

53    *spot* embroidered pattern of small flowers, fruits, and
      the like
60    *'Has* he has
      *confirmed* resolute, determined
66    *mammocked* tore to shreds
67    *on's* of his
69    *crack* young rascal
72    *will not out* will not go out
83    *Penelope* wife of Ulysses, king of Ithaca. During the
      long absence of her husband after the siege of Troy she
      was pressed to marry one of her many suitors. She put
      them off by pretending that she could not marry until
      she had finished a shroud she was weaving. At night
      she undid the work she had done in the day, so that the
      shroud was never completed.
85    *moths* (used with a double meaning: (1) the insects;
      (2) parasites, referring to the suitors of Penelope who
      lived in the house of Ulysses and consumed his goods)
86    *sensible* sensitive, capable of feeling
100-101  *They nothing doubt prevailing and to make it brief wars.*
      The sense of this passage is: 'They are confident of
      victory and that the campaign will be a short one.'
106   *disease our better mirth* spoil our pleasure, which will be
      better without her
110   *at a word* once for all


I.4   This scene opens the war with the Volsces which takes
      up the rest of the Act. The scene divisions, introduced
      by the eighteenth-century editors, are misleading, be-
      cause the action is continuous. The material is drawn
      largely from Plutarch (*Shakespeare's Plutarch*, pp.
      306-14).
4     *spoke* encountered
7     *Summon* call to a parley
9     *'larum* alarum, call to arms. Shakespeare uses these
      noises off stage to keep his audience aware of the other

battle between Cominius and the Volsces, which is taking place at the same time as the assault on Corioles

10     *Mars* (Roman god of war)

12     *fielded* in the battle-field

14–15   *No, nor a man that fears you less than he : | That's lesser than a little.* The sense is: 'No, and there is not a man here but fears you less than he does, if that is possible, since his fear of you is infinitesimal.' Shakespeare often intensifies the force of a negative by writing 'less' where modern usage would require 'more'. Compare *Troilus and Cressida* I.1.27–8:

> *Patience herself, what goddess e'er she be,*
> *Doth lesser blench at sufferance than I do.*

17     *pound us up* shut us up as in a pound (an enclosure for stray cattle, a pinfold)

20     *List* hark, listen to

21     *cloven* which is being cut to pieces

22     *our instruction* a lesson to us

       (stage direction) *the army of the Volsces* (the Volscian troops within the city who make an unexpected sally)

25     *proof* sound, impenetrable

29     (stage direction) *Alarum . . . cursing.* This stage direction, while calling for a battle of some length, fails to indicate what Martius does before he re-enters 'cursing', since he is given no exit. He must drive some of the Volsces off stage on the one side, while the rest of them press back the Romans on the other. It also leaves the activities and whereabouts of Titus Lartius obscure until he re-enters at line 49.

30     *contagion of the south.* The warm south and south-west winds brought mists which were thought to breed the plague – compare Caliban's curse on Prospero (*The Tempest*, I.2.323–4):

> *A south-west blow on ye*
> *And blister you all o'er !*

31  *You herd of – Boils.* The Folio reads: 'you Heard of Byles'. The broken sentence, together with the heavy use of alliteration running through this speech, gives a powerful impression of Martius's boiling rage.

32–3  *abhorred | Farther than seen* loathed (on account of your stink) before you are even in sight

36  *Pluto* (god of Hades, the classical hell)

38  *agued* shivering
    *Mend* do better
    *home* into the midst of the enemy

42  *Follow's!* Follow us! The Folio reads: 'As they vs to our Trenches followes.' This makes no sense, and many editors emend to 'followed'. It has also been suggested that 'followes' is a stage direction that has crept into the text. 'Follow's' is, however, a good colloquialism and carries on the sense and idiom of *Look to't. Come on!* in line 40.
    (stage direction) *Another alarum . . . shut in.* The Folio reads: 'Another Alarum, and Martius followes them to the gates, and is shut in.' This is a general account anticipating what is about to happen in the next seven lines, rather than a precise direction, but it would have its value for an actor about to be involved in an extended bout of hand-to-hand fighting. A more explicit stage direction follows at line 45.

43  *seconds* supporters

49  *To th'pot* to the stew-pot, referring to the way in which meat is cut up before being placed in it. The soldiers' slang is a sardonic comment on Martius's stirring call to action.

54  *answer* cope with, face

55  *sensibly* with his sensitive body
    *senseless* insensitive

56  *stand'st* thou standest
    *lost.* The Folio reads 'left', but the comparison that follows between Martius and a carbuncle (a red precious stone) demands 'lost'.

59     *Cato's.* The Folio reads: '*Calues*', an obvious mistake since Shakespeare is following North, who writes: 'For he was even such another as Cato would have a soldier and a captain to be' (*Shakespeare's Plutarch*, pp. 306–7). The Cato referred to is Cato the Censor, 234–149 B.C., who was not born until 250 years after Coriolanus's death.

64     *fetch him off* rescue him

      *make remain alike* stay with him, share his fate

I.5.3     *murrain* plague (literally a disease of cattle)

4     *movers* active men (ironical)

5     *drachma* (Greek coin of small value, worthless when cracked)

6     *Irons of a doit* weapons worth a farthing

      *hangmen.* The Elizabethan hangman was allowed to keep the clothes of his victims as a perquisite.

12     *make good* hold, secure

18     *physical* good for my health (blood-letting being the treatment in Shakespeare's day for all the ills that flesh is heir to)

21     *charms* magic spells

23     *Prosperity* success

23–4     *Thy friend no less | Than those* may she be no less a friend to thee than to those

I.6.1     *Breathe you* take a rest, catch your breath

      *are come off* have got clear

3     *retire* retreat

4     *struck* been striking blows

5     *By interims and conveying gusts* at intervals and by means of gusts of wind carrying the noise

6     *The Roman gods.* The sense is vocative.

7     *successes* fortunes

10    *issued* sallied forth

16    *briefly* a short time ago

17    *confound* waste

25    *tabor* small drum

29    *clip* embrace

32    *to bedward* toward bed, showing us the way to bed

36    *Ransoming him or pitying* releasing a man for ransom or
      remitting it out of pity

42    *He did inform the truth – but for our gentlemen* he told
      the truth – except in so far as our gentlemen were con-
      cerned. In the Folio the line runs: 'He did informe the
      truth: but for our Gentlemen,' a punctuation that has
      led many editors to take 'our gentlemen' as a sarcastic
      allusion to 'The common file'. It seems doubtful that
      Martius would, even in scorn, describe soldiers who
      had run away as 'gentlemen'. What happens is that with
      his customary respect for truth he comes to the support
      of the Messenger, and then recollects that he was
      seconded in his counter-attack by 'a few men' (*Shake-
      speare's Plutarch*, p. 306). Furthermore, it is most un-
      likely that he would not make an exception for Titus
      Lartius at least.

44-5  *budge | From* flinch from, give way before

53    *vaward* vanguard
      *Antiates* men of Antium (the chief city of the Volsces
      and the home of Aufidius) – the word is three-syllabled,
      as though written *Antiats*, which is the form it actually
      takes in the Folio at I.6.59.

55    *heart of hope* the man on whom all their hopes depend

60    *delay the present* make any delay now

61    *advanced* raised aloft

62    *prove* try the fortunes of

69-70 *fear | Lesser* fear less for

76    *O' me alone, make you a sword of me.* This is one of the
      most difficult passages in the play. The Folio reads:
      'Oh me alone, make you a sword of me:' – words which
      can be interpreted as expressive of surprise, protest, or

201

delight, and punctuated accordingly. The present editor's view is that Martius is enraptured to receive such a response – the rest of this speech is unusually courteous – and offers himself to the army as a sword to be made use of against the enemy.

77   *outward* insincere, superficial

78   *But is* that is not

83   *As cause will be obeyed* as circumstances require

84   *I shall.* The Folio reads: 'foure shall', but it is difficult to imagine Martius leaving the task of selection to four nameless men, especially when he has just said (line 81) that he intends to do it himself. Dover Wilson suggests that the capital 'I' in Shakespeare's handwriting might have been mistaken for the numeral '4'.
     *draw out* pick
     *command* troop, body of men

86   *ostentation* demonstration of enthusiasm

I.7   The stage direction with which the scene opens is in effect a summary of what follows. It may well represent part of the author's plot or scenario.

1   *ports* gates

3   *centuries* companies of the Roman army, each consisting originally of one hundred men

7   *guider* guide

I.8   The duel between Martius and Aufidius, to which this scene is devoted, is a Shakespearian addition to Plutarch's narrative.
     (stage direction) *at several doors* at different doors, from opposite sides of the stage

4   *fame and envy* hated fame

7   *Holloa* pursue with shouts

12   *of your bragged progeny* belonging to the ancestors you boast of. Aeneas, the legendary founder of the Roman

state, was, like Hector the scourge of the Greeks, a Trojan.

14    *Officious* meddling, giving unwanted assistance

15    *In your condemnèd seconds* by seconding me in such a damned cowardly fashion

I.9    (stage direction) *retreat* the trumpet call to bring back troops from the pursuit of the enemy

2    *Thou't* thou wouldst

4    *attend* listen
    *shrug* shrug their shoulders in disbelief

5    *admire* marvel

6    *gladly quaked* pleasurably agitated
    *dull* spiritless, stupid

7    *fusty* mouldy-smelling

10    *of* in the form of. Cominius means that the battle Martius has just taken part in was a mere snack in comparison with the large dinner (of fighting) that he had already eaten in Corioles.

12    *caparison* trappings (of a horse)

14    *charter* privilege, right

18    *effected his good will* carried out his intentions

19    *overta'en* surpassed (implying that Martius himself has not accomplished all that he set out to do)

22    *traducement* slander, calumny

24    *to the spire and top of praises vouched* proclaimed in the highest possible terms of praise

25    *but modest* only moderate praise

26    *sign* token

29    *not* not hear themselves remembered

30    *'gainst* when exposed to

31    *tent themselves with death* cure themselves by causing your death. A 'tent' was a roll of bandage used for probing wounds and for keeping them open in order to prevent their festering.

32    *good and good store* good in quality and plenty of them

35–6    *at | Your only choice* according to your own personal wishes, exactly as you choose

44    *Made all of false-faced soothing* given over entirely to hypocritical flattery

44–6    *When steel grows | Soft as the parasite's silk, let him be made | An overture for th'wars.* This is a difficult and much disputed passage. Assuming that *overture*, which frequently means an 'opening' in Elizabethan English, is here used for the man who makes the opening, the present editor interprets it thus: 'When arms and armour grow as soft as the court-parasite's silken clothes, let the parasite be made the spear-head of the attack.' Shakespeare probably had in mind two passages from North which he had just been using. In the first, Martius, in Corioles, finding himself surrounded by the enemy, 'made a lane through the midst of them'. In the second, leading his men against the Antiates, 'he made such a lane through them and opened a passage into the battle of the enemies' (*Shakespeare's Plutarch*, pages 308 and 310). Many editors emend *overture* to 'coverture', giving the sense 'let a covering of silk [instead of armour] be made for the parasite when he goes to war'.

47    *For that* because

48    *foiled* defeated

      *debile* feeble

      *without note* unnoticed

49    *shout me forth* cry me up

51    *little* slight achievement

51–2    *dieted | In* fattened on

52    *sauced* spiced, seasoned

54    *give* report

56    *means his proper harm* intends to commit suicide

61    *trim belonging* either 'fine trappings' or 'the equipment that goes with him', since each of these words can be taken as a noun or an adjective

65    *addition* title, mark of distinction

68     *fair* clean

71     *undercrest* support as if it were my crest, live up to

72     *To th'fairness of my power* as creditably as I can

76     *best* leading citizens

        *articulate* negotiate, come to terms

81     *lay* lodged

82     *used* treated. In North the man concerned is 'an honest wealthy man, and now a prisoner, who, living before in great wealth in his own country, liveth now a poor prisoner in the hands of his enemies' (*Shakespeare's Plutarch*, p. 312). By making the man poor Shakespeare increases an audience's sense of Martius's magnanimity and fundamental decency.

I.10     This little scene has a double function within the structure of the play as a whole. First, it has the effect of increasing the tension when, in IV.4, Coriolanus decides to enter Aufidius's house. Secondly, in showing Aufidius abandoning the ideals of honour and chivalrous emulation for the ways of treachery, it prepares for the *dénouement*.

2     *on good condition* on favourable terms

5     *be that I am* be one who refuses to accept defeat

6     *good condition* sound state, well-being. The word-play is an expression of Aufidius's bitterness.

7     *part that is at mercy* defeated side

14     *in an equal force* on fair terms

15     *potch* thrust, make a stab (a vulgar word for an action Aufidius recognizes as mean)

18     *stain* disgrace

19     *Shall fly out of itself* (it) shall change its nature

20     *naked* defenceless, without his sword

22     *Embarquements* embargoes, restraints

23     *rotten* corrupt with age, worn out

25     *upon my brother's guard* with my brother posted to protect him

26    *the hospitable canon* the law of hospitality

32–3    *that to the pace of it* | *I may spur on my journey* so that I may not be left behind by the speed of events

II.1    Serving as a link between the war with the Volsces, which is now over, and the struggle for power within Rome itself, which is about to begin, this scene is almost entirely of Shakespeare's own invention. In it he draws extensively on his knowledge and observation of London life. The houses and buildings described are wholly English, the crowd is a London crowd, and the Tribunes are depicted as self-important City magistrates. The baiting of them by Menenius is a piece of satirical comedy, contrasting strongly with the scenes of action which precede and follow it. It also reminds an audience of the class conflict with which the play began, and prepares them for its renewal.

1    *augurer* soothsayer, member of the Roman priesthood who studied omens

15    *enormity* irregularity of conduct, vice

19    *topping* surpassing

21    *censured* judged, thought of

22    *right-hand file* patricians (the right-hand file being the place of honour in the army in Shakespeare's day)

27–8    *a very little thief of occasion will rob you of a great deal of patience* the slightest pretext will make you extremely impatient

34–5    *wondrous single* extraordinarily feeble

36–8    *turn your eyes . . . selves* see yourselves as others see you

43    *known well enough* pretty notorious

45    *hot wine* wine made into a hot drink with the addition of sugar, spices, and so on, generally known as mulled wine (a popular drink in Elizabethan England)

46    *Tiber* the river on which Rome stands – here used for water generally

46–7    *something imperfect in favouring the first complaint* somewhat at fault for deciding cases too quickly in favour of the plaintiff, without waiting to hear the other side. Menenius is making a favourable contrast between his own expeditious handling of cases and the dilatory methods of the Tribunes which he describes later.

47     *tinder-like* inflammable, quick-tempered

48     *motion* cause, provocation

48–9     *converses more with the buttock of the night than with the forehead of the morning* is more used to staying up late at night than to rising early in the morning

50     *spend* get rid of

51     *wealsmen* men devoted to the public good, statesmen

52     *Lycurguses* wise legislators – Lycurgus being the legendary law-giver of Sparta

52–3     *if the drink you give me touch my palate adversely, I make a crooked face at it* if I do not like what you say, I show my displeasure in my looks

55–6     *the ass in compound with the major part of your syllables* a large element of the fool in most of what you say

58     *tell* say, relate

58–9     *the map of my microcosm* my face – since the face indicates by its expression what is going on within the little world of man, just as a globe shows the main features of the big world

60     *bisson conspectuities* blear-eyed insights. 'Conspectuities' is a nonce-word. Menenius is, to use a modern phrase, blinding the Tribunes with science. The Folio reads: 'beesome Conspectuities'.

61     *character* character-sketch. 'Characters' – in the sense of brief witty delineations of human types – were about to become something of a literary craze at the time when *Coriolanus* was written. The first book of Characters in English, Joseph Hall's *Characters of Vices and Virtues*, appeared in 1608.

64     *caps* doffing of caps as a mark of respect
        *legs* genuflections, bows

65     *wholesome* which might be spent more profitably

66     *cause* case in a court of law
       *orange-wife* woman who sells oranges
       *faucet-seller* one who sells taps for barrels
67     *rejourn* put off, postpone
68     *audience* hearing
69     *party and party* one litigant and another
70     *mummers* actors in a dumb show who conveyed their
       meaning by their facial expressions
70–71  *set up the bloody flag against* declare war on
72     *bleeding* unhealed, undecided
76–8   *a perfecter giber for the table than a necessary bencher in
       the Capitol* more successful as a wit at a dinner party
       than as a statesman dealing with national affairs
80     *subjects* (in two senses: (1) creatures; (2) topics)
83     *botcher* mender of old clothes
86     *Deucalion* (the counterpart in classical mythology, of
       Noah: survivor, along with his wife Pyrrha, of the
       Flood)
88     *Good-e'en.* A form of 'good even', this salutation means
       'good evening', but it was used at any time after noon.
       Compare *Romeo and Juliet*, II.4.107–10.
       *conversation* society
89     *being* you being, since you are. The use of a participle
       with a pronoun implied in a pronominal adjective (here
       'your' in 'your conversation') is fairly common in
       Shakespeare.
92     *the moon* Diana the goddess of chastity. Menenius's
       speech becomes courtly and complimentary when he
       addresses members of his own class, and especially
       ladies.
98–9   *prosperous approbation* confirmed success
109    *gives me an estate of* endows me with
110    *make a lip at* mock
111    *Galen* famous Greek physician (A.D. 129–199) – still
       regarded as an authority in Shakespeare's day
112    *empiricutic* quackish. This word, which appears in the
       Folio as 'Emperickqutique', is not to be found else-

where and seems to be a coinage of Menenius's. There would seem to be some proverbial basis for it, however, because George Herbert writes in his *Jacula Prudentum*: 'The words ending in *Ique* do mock the Physician (as Hectique, Paralitique, Apoplectique, Lethargique)' (No. 1044).

112    *to this preservative* compared with this means of preserving life and health

117    *Brings 'a* provided he brings

119    *On's brows*. Volumnia means that the sign of victory, the oaken garland, is on Coriolanus's head, not in his pocket.

121    *disciplined* thrashed

125    *An* if

126    *fidiused* treated as Aufidius was

127    *possessed* informed

130    *name* honour, credit

134    *purchasing* achieving

142–3    *stand for his place* be a candidate for the consulship. Volumnia has her son's career already planned for him, and sees his scars, which she reckons up so eagerly, as so many qualifications for office.

143    *Tarquin* (Tarquinius Superbus, the last king of Rome, who was expelled from the city and, when he attempted to win back his throne, was finally defeated at the battle of Lake Regillus about 496 B.C.)

153    *in's* in his (colloquial)
       *nervy* muscular, sinewy

154    *advanced* raised, uplifted; *declines* falls
       (stage direction) *sennet* notes on a trumpet or cornet to herald a stage procession
       *Titus Lartius*. Though he says nothing, Titus Lartius must be present in this scene, since Menenius refers at line 179 to 'three' (Cominius, Titus, and Coriolanus). Yet he has no right to be so, because he was left in Corioles at I.9.74–5 and he is still there at II.2.36 when the Senate decides to 'send for' him. It looks, therefore,

as though II.1, or at least this part of it, was composed at a different time from Act I and II.2.

157     *With fame* along with fame

         *to* in addition to

157–8   *these | In honour follows 'Coriolanus'.* The name Coriolanus follows these names as a mark of honour. North, who explains Roman nomenclature in detail, writes: 'The third [name] was some addition given, either for some act or notable service . . . or else for some special virtue they had' (*Shakespeare's Plutarch*, p. 313).

164     *prosperity* success

         (stage direction) *He kneels.* This stage direction, which appears as *Kneeles* in the Folio and is probably Shakespeare's own, emphasizes the right and proper relationship between mother and son. It was normal in Elizabethan England for a son to kneel when receiving his mother's blessing. The whole ceremony suffers a violent and shocking reversal in V.3 where Volumnia kneels to her son.

166     *deed-achieving honour* honour won by deeds

168     *gracious* lovely

177     *light and heavy* joyful and sad

182     *grafted to your relish* implanted with a liking for you

190     *change of honours* new honours or titles

191     *inherited* realized, taken possession of. Volumnia sees her son as the heir who has come into the estate and titles that she had long hoped would be his.

196     *sway with* rule over. Coriolanus's answer to Volumnia marks the beginning of the rift between the mother, who has her son's future all mapped out for him, and the son himself, who wishes to go his own way.

197     *sights* eyes

199     *rapture* fit

200     *chats* gossips about

         *kitchen malkin* slatternly kitchen-maid

201     *lockram* piece of hempen fabric

         *reechy* dirty, grimy

202 *bulks* wooden projections in front of Elizabethan shops, used for displaying wares

203 *leads* lead-covered roofs; *ridges horsed* ridges (on the roofs of houses) covered with spectators sitting astride them as though on horseback

204 *variable complexions* all sorts of people

205 *Seld-shown flamens* priests rarely seen in public

207 *vulgar station* place in the crowd

209 *nicely gawded* skilfully made-up
   *spoil* ravages

210 *Phoebus* the sun. In Shakespeare's day sun-burn was not fashionable.
   *pother* fuss, turmoil

213 *posture* bearing

216 *temperately transport* carry in a balanced, self-controlled manner

217 *From where he should begin and end* from the right beginning to the proper conclusion

218–20 *Doubt not . . . forget* be sure that the commoners, whom we represent, will, because of their long-standing hostility to him, forget

223 *As* as that

226 *napless* threadbare

229 *miss* go without

230 *carry* win, obtain
   *but* except

234 *as our good wills* as our interest demands

236 *To him, or our authority's for an end.* In the Folio this line runs: 'To him, or our Authorities, for an end.' Most editors emend as follows: 'To him or our authorities. For an end,' taking 'For an end' to mean 'To this end'. As compared with this change of punctuation and sense, the reading adopted involves a minimum of interference with the text and makes good sense, *for* meaning 'on the way to, destined for' as in 'we are for the dark' (*Antony and Cleopatra*, V.2.193).

237 *suggest* insinuate to

211

238     *still* always

240     *Dispropertied* deprived of their essential nature, made a farce of

243     *provand* provender

247     *teach* lecture (as Coriolanus did in I.1). Many editors emend to 'touch': that is, touch to the quick, inflame.

247–8     *which time shall not want,* | *If he be put upon*'*t* which time will surely come, if he is provoked into doing it

249–50     *his fire* | *To kindle their dry stubble* the spark setting him alight that will then kindle those who are like dry stubble. The language is very compact, but the main idea is clear enough: both Coriolanus and the people are extremely inflammable.

258     *Jove* Jupiter (chief god of the Romans)

261–2     *carry with us ears and eyes for th'time,* | *But hearts for the event* see and hear what passes, but keep our hearts fixed on our purpose

II.2     This scene is built on a striking contrast between the quiet opening, with its shrewd appraisals of Coriolanus's character and of his attitude towards the people, and the pomp and circumstance of the public ceremony that follows.

5     *vengeance* frightfully

7     *hath* often emended, unnecessarily, to 'have'. The use of 'there is', 'there hath', etc., before a plural subject is very common in Shakespeare.

13     *in* of

14     *carelessness* indifference to public opinion

16     *waved indifferently* would be wavering impartially

19     *discover him their opposite* reveal him as their opponent

20     *to seem to affect* to give the impression of cultivating

24     *degrees* steps

26–7     *bonneted, without . . . report* went cap-in-hand and, without doing anything else whatever to earn it, won immediate popularity

34 (stage direction) *Lictors* attendants on the Roman magistrates. In the Folio this stage direction ends with the
words: '*Coriolanus stands*', but this must be wrong,
since at line 64 comes the explicit direction, supported
by the dialogue, '*Coriolanus rises, and offers to go away*'.

35 *determined of* settled about

38 *gratify* show our gratitude for

39 *stood for* defended

42 *well-found* fortunate

45 *remember* acknowledge our debt to

47-9 *make us think . . . stretch it out* cause us to feel that our
state has not the means to repay him fully rather than
that we are unwilling to strain those means to the
utmost

51 *Your loving motion toward* your kind influence with

52 *yield* assent to
*convented* convened, met

53 *treaty* proposal for an agreement

56 *blessed* happy, glad

58 *off* off the point, irrelevant

63 *tie* oblige, constrain

64 (stage direction) *offers* makes ready, prepares, tries

69 *disbenched* unseated, caused to rise

71 *soothed* flattered

72 *as they weigh* according to their worth

75 *monstered* turned into marvels

80-120 *I shall lack voice. The deeds of Coriolanus . . . To ease his
breast with panting.* Cominius's formal oration, or *laus*,
of Coriolanus is one of the finest pieces of epic poetry
in English. Its basic assumption, which is also that of
epic, is contained in the sentence: 'It is held . . . haver.'
This derives almost literally from Plutarch, who writes:
'Now in those days valiantness was honoured in Rome
above all other virtues; which they call *virtus*, by the
name of virtue itself, as including in that general name
all other special virtues besides' (*Shakespeare's Plutarch*,
p. 297).

85   *singly counterpoised* equalled by any other individual

86   *made a head for* raised an army against

87   *Beyond the mark* beyond the reach, beyond the powers

89   *Amazonian chin* beardless chin – the Amazons being female warriors in classical myth

93   *on his knee* on to his knee

94   *act the woman in the scene* take the female part in the action, like the boy-actors of the Elizabethan stage

95   *meed* reward

96-7   *His pupil age* | *Man-entered thus* having started his apprenticeship in the style of one who had already completed it

99   *lurched all swords of the garland* robbed all other soldiers of their glory, stole the show

101   *speak him home* find words to do him justice

105   *stem* prow

      *stamp* tool or die for stamping a mark or design on some softer material

106-7   *took . . . foot.* | *He . . . blood.* The Folio reads: 'tooke from face to foot: | He was a thing of Blood,' which most editors emend to 'took; from face to foot | He was a thing of blood,'. To the present editor the alteration seems unnecessary, since the passage has much in common with, and appears to have grown out of, the speech of the Bloody Sergeant in I.2 of *Macbeth*. The action described in the words 'it took from face to foot' is the same as that of Macbeth when he fought Macdonwald 'Till he unseamed him from the nave to the chops', except that the movement of the sword is downwards, not upwards.

106   *took* (double meaning: (1) made an impression; (2) destroyed)

108   *timed with* regularly accompanied by

109   *mortal* fatal (because it seemed death to enter it)

109-10   *which he painted* | *With shunless destiny. which* refers to the city rather than to the gates, while *shunless destiny* is probably the *memento mori*, the bony representation of death, which was such a common motif in the Art of the Middle Ages and the Renaissance, especially from about the beginning of the fifteenth century to the middle of the seventeenth. In *Measure for Measure* Shakespeare writes (III.1.11–13):

> *Merely thou art Death's fool;*
> *For him thou labourest by thy flight to shun*
> *And yet run'st toward him still.*

111     *reinforcement* fresh assault

111–12     *struck | Corioles like a planet* blasted it. Planets were believed to be capable of exerting a malignant influence, and the planet involved here is indubitably Mars.

112–13     *Now all's his, | When* no sooner is all his than

114     *ready sense* hearing alert for the sound of battle
       *doubled* twice as strong as before

115     *Requickened* revived, reanimated
       *fatigate* weary

117     *reeking* steaming (like a stream of blood)

118     *spoil* massacre

119     *stood* stood still, stopped

120     *Worthy* heroic, deserving the highest praise

121     *He cannot but with measure fit* he cannot help but measure up to

125     *misery* utter poverty

127     *To spend the time to end it* to spend his life in doing great actions, which to him is an end in itself

135     *naked* exposed to view

137     *pass* omit

138     *voices* votes

139     *Put them not to't* don't press them too hard

142     *your form* the form which custom prescribes to you

142–3     *It is a part | That I shall blush in acting.* From this point onwards, down to the end of Act III, the feeling that he is playing a shameful role, instead of being his own true self, is constantly with Coriolanus.

148 *stand upon't* make an issue of it, insist on it

150 *purpose* proposal

154 *require* make his request of them

155 *what* that what

II.3 With this scene the great central section of the play, dealing with the clash between Coriolanus and the people, begins. The material on which it is based comes from North (*Shakespeare's Plutarch*, pp. 317–20) but Shakespeare alters it radically. In the source Coriolanus shows no reluctance about appearing in the market-place and exhibiting his wounds to the citizens. The reluctance is on their side; but after he had shown them his scars:

> there was not a man among the people but was ashamed of himself to refuse so valiant a man. And one of them said to another:
>> 'We must needs choose him Consul; there is no remedy.'

Nevertheless, he fails to secure the consulship, because on the day of the election:

> the love and good-will of the common people turned straight to an hate and envy toward him, fearing to put this office of sovereign authority into his hands, being a man somewhat partial toward the nobility and of great credit and authority amongst the patricians, and as one they might doubt would take away altogether the liberty from the people.

There is no suggestion in Plutarch that the people have been manipulated by their Tribunes.

1 *Once* once for all, in a word

13–14 *a little help will serve* it will not need much effort on our part

15 *stuck not* did not hesitate

18 *abram* dark brown

21-2  *their consent of one direct way* their agreement to go in one direction

31  *rotten* unhealthy, corrupting (compare I.4.30, and note)

33-4  *You may* go on, have your little joke

36  *that's no matter, the greater part carries it* that doesn't matter: the vote need not be unanimous; a majority is enough

42  *by particulars* to individuals, one by one

47  *you are not right* you are mistaken

55  *think upon* think kindly of. This phrase – badly chosen by the normally diplomatic Menenius – was part of the Elizabethan beggar's patter and, as such, it rankles with Coriolanus.

56-7  *like the virtues | Which our divines lose by 'em* as they forget the virtuous precepts which our priests throw away on them

59  (stage direction) *Enter three of the Citizens.* There is some confusion here. The stage direction demands three Citizens and there are three parts, though the First Citizen has only one brief speech. On the other hand, Coriolanus describes them as 'a brace' when they first appear, and as they go he remarks 'There's in all two worthy voices begged', from which it would seem that only two Citizens were intended to be on the stage.

65  *Ay, but not mine.* The Folio reads: 'I, but mine'. The Third Citizen's question in the next line makes it clear that the word 'not' has been omitted.

73  *The price is to ask it kindly.* This answer throws a great deal of light on Shakespeare's attitude to the citizens – one of them at least can give Coriolanus a lesson in manners. For the political significance of 'kindly' see Introduction, pp. 29-30.

79  *A match* a bargain, agreed!

84  *stand* agree

90-92  *You have been a scourge . . . common people.* The Fourth Citizen is the only one who makes any attempt to employ the tactics which, as Brutus reveals later in the scene, the Tribunes had instructed the people to use.

94   *common* cheap, promiscuous

96   *condition* form of behaviour
     *gentle* aristocratic, gentleman-like

99   *be off to them* raise my hat to them

100  *bewitchment* enchanting manners
     *popular man* demagogue, one who curries popular favour

107  *seal* confirm

112–23 *Better it is to die . . . will I do.* Coriolanus's sarcasms, which the citizens fail to understand, and his refusal to show his wounds, reveal how unbearable the whole business is becoming to him. Left alone for a few moments, he expresses his outraged feelings in a soliloquy which acquires added bite from the use of heroic couplets, the vehicle of satire.

114  *wolvish toge* toga which makes me look like a wolf (in sheep's clothing). The Folio reads: 'Wooluish tongue'. It seems probable that the compositor, finding the unfamiliar word 'toge' in the manuscript, read it as 'tõge': that is, the abbreviated form of 'tongue'.

115  *Hob and Dick.* This was the equivalent of 'Tom, Dick and Harry'. 'Hob' was the rustic version of 'Robert'.
     *that does appear* who make their appearance

116  *needless vouches* formal confirmations that are unnecessary, since he has already been appointed by the Senate

118  *antique time* old-fashioned institutions

120  *to o'erpeer* to be able to see over the top of it

126  *Watched* done guard duty

138  *limitation* appointed time

139  *Endue* endow

144  *upon your approbation* to ratify your election

172  *no further with you* no further use for you

173  *ignorant to see't* too simple-minded to see it

176  *lessoned* instructed. It is by touches like this that Shakespeare extends the whole scope of the play. An

audience is made aware that an intensive course of political indoctrination (of which they have seen nothing) has been given to the people by the Tribunes.

180 *body of the weal* commonwealth
*arriving* reaching, attaining to

183 *plebeii* plebeians

186 *stood for* was a candidate for

188 *Translate* change, transform

190 *touched* tested the quality of

193 *As cause had called you up* when some crisis had aroused you

195 *article* any condition or stipulation

199 *free* frank, undisguised

203 *heart* courage. The idea of the heart as the seat of counsel is also relevant.
*cry* protest

204 *rectorship* rule, governance

204–7 *Have you . . . tongues?* Have you before this occasion denied your votes to a man who asked for them in the right way, and do you now bestow them on one who mocked instead of asking?

211 *piece* add to, eke out

217 *safer* sounder

218 *Enforce* stress, make a point of

219 *forget not* do not fail to mention

220 *weed* garment, apparel

223 *apprehension* perception, ability to understand the meaning of
*portance* behaviour

227 *No impediment between* provided that no hitch occurred in the interim

234 *read lectures* gave lessons

237–44 *The noble house . . . ancestor.* This passage is a paraphrase of the opening words of Plutarch's *Life* (*Shakespeare's Plutarch*, p. 296). There is a fine irony in the fact that the information about Coriolanus's noble origins is given by his enemies as part of their plot to ruin him.

242-4 *And Censorinus, nobly namèd so, | Twice being by the people chosen censor, | Was his great ancestor.* The Folio reads:

> *And Nobly nam'd, so twice being Censor,*
> *Was his great Ancestor.*

It is plain that something has been omitted, and editors have supplied the missing words from North. An alternative reconstruction is:

> *And Censorinus that was so surnamed*
> *And nobly namèd so, . . .*

243 *censor* (important Roman magistrate, who maintained the official list of citizens and controlled public morals)

248 *Scaling* weighing

250 *sudden* hasty

251 *putting on* instigation

252 *presently* immediately
*drawn your number* collected a crowd

255 *put in hazard* ventured

256 *Than stay, past doubt, for greater* than wait for the chance of a bigger and surer one

258-9 *observe and answer | The vantage of his anger* look out for and take full advantage of the opportunity his anger will provide

III.1 This important scene, in which the political divisions in Rome come to a head, is based on North (*Shakespeare's Plutarch*, pp. 320–27). Shakespeare, however, enriches the original enormously by adding a fine ironical opening of his own. Knowing nothing of the activities of the Tribunes, Coriolanus and those about him take it for granted that he is now Consul and behave as though his term of office had already begun. At the

moment when he is about to be confronted with civil
disorder and to be tested as a statesman, the hero is
wholly taken up with Aufidius and the Volsces.

1     *made new head* raised a fresh army

3     *swifter composition* coming to terms the more quickly

5     *road* inroads, incursions

6     *worn* worn down, exhausted

7     *ages* lifetimes

9     *On safeguard* under safe-conduct

16     *To hopeless restitution* beyond all hope of recovery
      *so* provided that, so that

19–20   *I wish I had a cause to seek him there, | To oppose his
hatred fully* (a pregnant piece of unconscious irony)

23     *prank them* dress themselves up, flaunt themselves

24     *Against all noble sufferance* beyond the endurance of the
nobility

29     *passed* been approved by

36     *rule* control

43     *repined* complained, expressed regret

47     *sithence* since

48     *You are like to do such business.* The present edition
follows the Folio in assigning this speech to Cominius.
Many editors give it to Coriolanus on the grounds that
the abbreviated names used in the Folio (*Cor.* and *Com.*)
are easily confused and that Brutus's answer is directed
to Coriolanus. It could, however, be equally intended
for Coriolanus's party.

48–9   *Not unlike | Each way to better yours* likely to make a
better job of providing for the welfare of the state than
you are

52     *that* that arrogance

55     *are out of* have strayed from

58     *abused* misled, deceived
      *paltering* trickery, equivocation

60–61   *dishonoured rub* dishonourable obstacle; *laid falsely*
treacherously placed; *plain way* level track. All three
images are taken from the game of bowls.

65    *For* as for

66    *meiny* multitude, crowd

67–8  *Regard me ... themselves* take note that I am no
      flatterer, so that in what I say they will really see them-
      selves as they are

70    *cockle* tares, darnel. Shakespeare found this word in
      North (*Shakespeare's Plutarch*, p. 322) and it suggested
      to him the parable of the wheat and the tares in
      the Bible (Matthew 13.24–30) which he uses in lines
      71–2.

78    *till their decay* till death
      *measles* (punning on: (1) the disease; (2) scabs, scurvy
      wretches)

79    *tetter* cover the skin with scabs. Compare *Hamlet*,
      I.5.71–3:

> *And a most instant tetter barked about,*
> *Most lazar-like, with vile and loathsome crust,*
> *All my smooth body.*

85    *patient* calm

89    *Triton* (minor sea-god who served as trumpeter to
      Neptune)

90    *from the canon* out of order, unconstitutional. Cominius's
      point is that the Tribunes can only express the will of
      the people; they have no right to lay down the law.
      Coriolanus expands the same idea in his speech that
      follows.

91    *O good.* The Folio reads: 'O God!' which gives a pos-
      sible sense but not the parallel that seems to be required
      by 'grave but reckless' in line 92.

93    *Hydra* many-headed monster of Greek myth. When
      one of its heads was cut off, two more replaced it.

95    *horn* wind instrument of that name
      *o'th'monster's* of the monster – Shakespeare sometimes
      uses the double genitive.

96    *turn your current in a ditch* divert your stream (of
      power) into a ditch

97–8   *If he have power,* | *Then vail your ignorance* if this man really has power, let your negligence that gave it him vail (or bow down) before him

99   *learned* wise

101   *have cushions by you* sit beside you in the Senate

103–4   *When, both your voices blended, the great'st taste* | *Most palates theirs* when the voices of the plebeians are blended with those of the senators, the dominant flavour of the compound will taste more of populace than of Senate

106   *popular* plebeian
     *bench* Senate, governing body

109   *up* in action, exerting power

110   *confusion* chaos

111–12   *take* | *The one by th'other* use one to destroy the other

114   *as 'twas used* as was customary

120   *more worthier.* Compare IV.7.8 and note.

121   *our recompense* our reward to them for services done

122   *Being pressed* when they were conscripted

123   *navel* nerve centre
     *touched* threatened

124   *thread* pass through one by one

129   *All cause unborn* utterly without justification
     *native* origin

130   *frank* generous

131   *bosom multiplied* multiple stomach, the stomach of the many-headed monster

134   *greater poll* larger number of heads, majority

137   *cares* concern for the state

142   *Seal* confirm
     *double worship* divided sovereignty

144   *Insult* behave insolently
     *without* beyond
     *gentry* high birth

145   *conclude* come to a decision

146   *omit* neglect, disregard

148   *slightness* trifling, vacillation

148–9   *Purpose so barred ... purpose* when sound policy is so obstructed, it follows that nothing effective is accomplished

152     *doubt* fear

154     *To jump a body with a dangerous physic* to risk giving a dangerous treatment to a body

156     *The multitudinous tongue* those who speak for the multitude, the Tribunes

157     *The sweet* the sweets of office

159     *integrity* unity, wholeness

162     *answer* answer for it

163     *despite* scorn, contempt

164     *bald* witless (as well as hairless)

166     *th'greater bench* the Senate

167     *When what's not meet, but what must be, was law* when that which was not right, but which was nevertheless unavoidable, was made law

169     *Let what is meet be said it must be meet* let it be said that the right thing to do shall be done

172     *Aediles* (subordinate officials who assisted the Tribunes)

174     *Attach* arrest
        *innovator* revolutionary

176     *answer* interrogation, trial

177     *surety* go bail for

180     *respect* thought, consideration

185–8   *Tribunes! Patricians! Citizens! What ho! ... out of breath.* The Folio assigns lines 185–6 to *2 Sen.*, line 187 to *All.* and line 188 to *Mene.* It is clear, however, that lines 185–6 must belong to the mixed crowd of patricians and citizens. The allocation of line 187 is doubtful. In this edition it is given to Menenius, because he is the only person interested in peace and because his uttering it adds further point to his statement, 'I am out of breath.'

189     *speak* make a speech

193     *at point to lose* on the point of losing

205     *distinctly ranges* is clearly arranged in a definite order. Shakespeare is probably thinking of the courses of

brick or stone which go to make up a building. Compare 'the wide arch of the ranged empire' (*Antony and Cleopatra*, I.1.33-4). But implicit in the image is the Elizabethan idea of the hierarchical state, which is in grave danger at this point.

211     *present* immediate

212     *th'rock Tarpeian*. The Tarpeian rock was a cliff on the Capitoline hill in Rome from which traitors were thrown headlong down.

228     (stage direction) *beat in* driven off the stage

230     *naught* lost, ruined

230-31     *Stand fast! | We have as many friends as enemies.* The Folio gives this speech to *Com.* The difficulty about this assignment is that at lines 244-9 Cominius is in favour of retreat, not of fighting. Coriolanus alone wants to make a stand.

234     *cause* disease, illness

235     *tent* treat, cure

236     *Come, sir, along with us.* The Folio gives this line to *Corio.* but he must be the character addressed, not the speaker.

237-41     *I would they were barbarians, as they are . . . another.* The Folio assigns all these lines to *Mene.*, which is a palpable mistake. The first three are in the idiom of Coriolanus, and, unless he speaks them, there is no point in Menenius's plea, 'Put not your worthy rage into your tongue.'

241     *One time will owe another* another time will pay for this

243     *Take up* take on, cope with

244     *'tis odds beyond arithmetic* their numbers are infinitely greater than ours

245-6     *stands | Against a falling fabric* resists (that is, tries to prop up) a falling building

247     *tag* rabble

248     *o'erbear* overwhelm

255     *Neptune* the god of the sea in classical mythology. He was armed with a trident (or three-pronged spear).

256     *His heart's his mouth* he speaks what he feels

271     *sure on't* for certain

273-4   *Do not cry havoc, where you should but hunt | With modest warrant* do not call for indiscriminate slaughter in a case where your licence to hunt is strictly limited. The situation is now the reverse of that which existed in I.1, where Coriolanus thought of himself as the hunter and of the people as the quarry.

275     *holp* helped

       *make this rescue.* To 'make rescue' was a technical term in English law, meaning to use force in order to release a man from custody – a very serious offence.

284     *peremptory* determined, resolved

286     *our danger.* The Folio reads 'one danger', but the sense demands the contrast between 'our danger' and 'our death'.

290     *deservèd* deserving, meritorious

302     *clean kam* quite wrong, utterly misleading

304-6   *The service of the foot . . . was.* The Folio assigns these words to Menenius, but he has already made the point (lines 294-5) that the diseased limb (Coriolanus) can be cured. Gangrene, however, is incurable and requires amputation of the affected limb, which is precisely what Menenius wishes to avoid. The lines are, in fact, the logical continuation of Sicinius's remark at line 293, 'He's a disease that must be cut away.'

311     *unscanned swiftness* unthinking haste

312     *to's* to its

       *process* proper form of law

320     *bolted* refined, carefully considered. To 'bolt' meal was to pass it through a sieve or cloth in order to separate the flour from the bran.

323-4   *answer by a lawful form, | In peace, to his utmost peril* stand his trial peacefully even though his life be at stake

III.2     For Coriolanus this scene is critical, for he finds himself faced with a conflict of loyalties. It owes practically nothing to Plutarch, who merely says that at this juncture the patricians were divided, their younger members being intransigent while 'the most ancient Senators' favoured some sort of compromise with the people (*Shakespeare's Plutarch*, pp. 330–31).

4       *precipitation* headlong drop, precipice

5       *Below the beam of sight* farther than the eye can reach

7       *I muse* I wonder, I am puzzled

9       *woollen vassals* slaves clad in coarse woollens

9–10    *things created | To buy and sell with groats* born to be mere petty traders

12      *ordinance* rank

18      *Let go* enough! desist!

21      *crossings*. The Folio reads 'things', which is unmetrical and makes no sense. The emendation accepted by most editors, 'thwartings', is not a word that is to be found elsewhere in Shakespeare's work as a noun. C. J. Sisson suggests 'taxings' as graphically probable. 'Crossings' is good Shakespearian English – Glendower tells Hotspur, 'Cousin, of many men | I do not bear these crossings' (*1 Henry IV*, III.1.35–6) – and it links up with the verb *to cross* in line 23, just as *dispositions* links up with *disposed* in line 22.

23      *Ere they lacked power* while they still had power, before they lost power

29      *apt* yielding, compliant

32      *stoop to th'heart*. Most editors emend 'heart', which is the reading of the Folio, to 'herd'. But *stoop to th'heart*, meaning 'humble his very inmost self', makes good sense and anticipates Coriolanus's own words at lines 99–101, 'Must I | With my base tongue give to my noble heart | A lie that it must bear?' The Folio reading points straight to the central issue of this scene: whether Coriolanus will preserve his essential nobility of spirit intact or not.

33      *fit* madness; *physic* medicine, medical treatment

39–41   *You are too absolute . . . say*. The Folio reads:

> *You are too absolute,*
> *Though therein you can neuer be too Noble,*
> *But when extremities speake. I haue heard you say,*

Many editors accept the Folio text as it stands, taking *But when* to mean 'except when'. This, however, is not Volumnia's point. What she is saying is that when it comes to the push, as she has heard Coriolanus himself admit, honour and policy can be reconciled.

39    *absolute* intransigent

41    *extremities speak* absolute necessity demands

42    *policy* stratagems

       *unsevered* inseparable

51    *stands in like request* is equally requisite

       *force* urge

52    *lies you on* is incumbent on you

53    *instruction* prompting, manner expressive of your feelings

55    *roted* learned by rote and spoken with no sincerity

57    *Of no allowance* bearing no valid relationship

59    *take in* capture

64    *I am* I represent, I speak for

68    *inheritance* obtaining, winning

69    *that want* that failure to fawn

71    *Not* not only

72–86  *I prithee now, my son … person.* This speech, which calls for a great deal of appropriate gesture, since Volumnia is showing her son how to behave as well as telling him what to say, must have been a great opportunity for the boy-actor who first played the part. For the modern editor, however, it offers some puzzles, since it is one long involved sentence, liberally sprinkled with parentheses.

73    *this bonnet* (the cap on his head, which she either points to or possibly removes and handles)

74    *be with them* comply with their wish, get round them

75      *bussing* kissing. At this point Volumnia demonstrates how to curtsey.

76      *Action* gesture

77–80  The Folio reads as follows:

> *wauing thy head,*
> *Which often thus correcting thy stout heart,*
> *Now humble as the ripest Mulberry,*
> *That will not hold the handling : or say to them,*

The only way to make any sense of this as it stands is to regard *Which* as referring to *thy head* and to take *humble* as a verb in the imperative. Even so *or* is redundant, since Volumnia is not recommending alternative courses of action but one single procedure in which gesture is succeeded by speech. In this edition, therefore, *or* is omitted and *Which* emended to *With*.

77      *waving thy head* (moving your head up and down in sign of repentance)

78      *thus*. Here Volumnia beats her breast or makes some such gesture of self-chastisement.

85      *theirs* according to their wishes

91      *in a fiery gulf* into a fiery pit or chasm

94      *make strong party* gather a strong faction about you

99      *unbarbed sconce* uncovered head (a sign of great respect)

102    *plot* piece of earth (that is, his body)

103    *mould* (used in two senses: (1) form; (2) earth)

106    *discharge to th'life* play convincingly

113    *choired with* sang in tune with

114    *Small* high-pitched

115    *babies lulls* lulls dolls

116    *Tent* lodge, encamp

        *take up* fill up

117    *glasses of my sight* eyeballs

123    *inherent* fixed, irremovable

127    *Thy dangerous stoutness* the danger created by your obstinacy

130    *owe* own, possess. Volumnia means that Coriolanus's

pride is of his own making (she has had no part in it!) and he must take the responsibility for it.

132    *mountebank* win by trickery and the use of patter

133    *Cog* swindle, wheedle. Coriolanus's use of words like this is expressive of the self-disgust he feels at agreeing to act like a cheap-jack.

143    *by invention* with trumped-up charges


III.3    Based largely on North (*Shakespeare's Plutarch*, pp. 325–33), this scene is the climax of the struggle for political power in Rome. Shakespeare heightens the effect of it all in two ways: first, by giving greater prominence to the care and deliberation with which the Tribunes make their arrangements for the organization of the crowd; secondly, by making Coriolanus far more defiant and vociferous than he is in Plutarch, where he is taken by surprise and merely seeks to excuse himself.

3    *Enforce him* ply him hard
     *envy* malice, hatred

9    *voices* cries in chorus, claque

10    *by th'poll* according to the list of voters. For a full discussion of the voting procedure at this point in the play, see Geoffrey Bullough's *Narrative and Dramatic Sources of Shakespeare*, vol. v, pp. 466–70. The voting was, in fact, by tribes (as is indicated in line 11), a method that was bound to give the plebeians a majority; but Shakespeare was misled by North, who, following the French of Amyot, adds some detail which does not appear at all in Plutarch's Greek. After relating how the Tribunes insisted that the voting should be by tribes, North continues: 'for by this means the multitude of the poor needy people . . . came to be of greater force, because their voices were numbered by the poll' (*Shakespeare's Plutarch*, pp. 331–2). The final clause in this sentence, for which there is no equivalent in Plutarch, seems to have given Shakespeare the impression that

the method of voting was the same as that adopted at an English parliamentary election, where heads were counted, and where the volume of noise created in support of a candidate appears to have carried at least as much weight as the number of votes cast for him. See J. E. Neale, *The Elizabethan House of Commons*, Penguin Books edition, Harmondsworth, 1963, pp. 81–2.

12    *presently* immediately

18    *i'th' truth o'th' cause* in the justice of the case. For an audience in 1608 or thereabouts these words would probably have had a distinctly Puritan ring.

26–7   *have his worth | Of contradiction* have his pennyworth of answering back (that is, give as good as he gets). The phrase may well be a memory of Philemon Holland's translation of *The Romane Historie of T. Livy* (1600). There Livy writes that the Commons complained that they had no hope of food and sustenance, 'unlesse the Tribunes be delivered and yeelded prisoners hand and foot bound to *C. Martius*, unlesse he might have his penniworths of the backe and shoulders of the commons of Rome' (*Narrative and Dramatic Sources of Shakespeare*, ed. Geoffrey Bullough, vol. v, p. 501).

29    *looks* promises, looks likely

32    *piece* piece of money, coin

33    *bear the knave by th'volume* put up with being called knave to any extent

36    *shows* ceremonies

40    *Audience!* attention!

42    *this present* the matter in hand. North writes (*Shakespeare's Plutarch*, p. 331):

> *Martius . . . said that thereupon he did willingly offer himself to the people, to be tried upon that accusation . . . 'conditionally', quoth he, 'that you charge me with nothing else besides'. They promised they would not.*

43    *determine* end, be settled

45    *Allow* acknowledge the authority of

57     *envy you* show ill will towards you

64     *seasoned* established, mature

       *wind* insinuate (a charge that comes well from the Tribunes!)

68     *fold in* envelop, enfold

69     *their traitor* traitor to them

       *injurious* insultingly libellous

81     *capital* punishable by death

85     *You!* Coriolanus's contempt springs from the fact that 'service' to him means only military service.

97     *not* not only

102    *precipitation* being thrown

114    *estimate* reputation, honour

120    *cry* pack

121    *reek* foggy vapours

124–33 *And here remain with your uncertainty! | . . . won you without blows.* Here, perhaps, are to be seen the first glimmerings, as yet incompletely formulated, of the hero's decision to turn against Rome.

129    *finds not till it feels* foresees nothing until it experiences it

130–31 *Making but reservation of yourselves | Still your own foes* leaving none in the city except yourselves who are always your own worst enemies

132    *abated* humbled, abject

135    (stage direction) *Exeunt Coriolanus . . . Patricians.* The Folio reads: '*Exeunt Coriolanus, Cominius, with Cumalijs*', the compositor having apparently mistaken *cum aliis*, the Latin for 'with the others', for a personal name.

140    *vexation* torment of mind, mortification. In this moment of triumph Sicinius's customary political sagacity deserts him. The advice he gives to the people is taken, and the manner in which Coriolanus is hooted out of the city rankles deeply with him and helps to inspire his determination to be revenged.

IV.1  Nowhere else in the play does Coriolanus appear to better advantage than in this scene of leave-taking which is developed out of a few lines in North, relating how he took 'his leave of his mother and wife, finding them weeping and shrieking out for sorrow, and ... comforted and persuaded them to be content with his chance' (*Shakespeare's Plutarch*, p. 333).

3–9  *You were used ... cunning.* The same sentiments, expressed in much greater detail, are to be found in *Troilus and Cressida*, I.3.17–54.

4  *extremities was* great crises were

7–9  *fortune's blows | When most struck home, being gentle wounded craves | A noble cunning.* The syntax is loose – as it often is in colloquial speech – but the sense comes through: 'when fortune strikes her hardest blows, one needs the training of a gentleman to take them as a gentleman should'.

11  *conned* studied, learned by heart

13  *the red pestilence* (probably typhus, which caused a red eruption of the skin)

15  *lacked* missed

17  *Hercules* (the most popular hero of classical mythology, who carried out twelve stupendous 'labours' or tasks)

26  *fond* foolish

27  *wot* know

29  *Believe't not lightly* believe firmly, be assured of this

32  *or exceed the common* either do something exceptional

33  *cautelous* crafty, deceitful
    *practice* stratagems

36  *wild exposture* rash exposure of yourself

37  *O the gods!* The Folio assigns this exclamation to *Corio.* but the words are in the idiom of Virgilia (compare line 12).

41  *repeal* recall

49  *of noble touch* of proved nobility (like gold that has passed the test of the touchstone)

55–7  *If I could shake off but one seven years ... foot.* A nice touch that is very much in character – Coriolanus's exile has made Menenius feel seven years older, just as his triumph made him feel seven years younger at II.1.109–11.

IV.2 In keeping with the symmetrical structure of the play, this scene, which brings the central part of the action to a close, is like a mirror-image of II.1, the scene with which this part of the action began. At the end of II.1 the Tribunes, fearing Coriolanus, were laying plans for his overthrow; at the opening of this scene those plans have been successful. At the beginning of II.1 Menenius was baiting the Tribunes; at the end of this scene Volumnia is cursing them. Like II.1, it owes nothing to Plutarch.

16 *mankind.* Sicinius uses the word in the sense of 'mad' (compare *The Winter's Tale,* II.3.67, where Leontes calls Paulina 'A mankind witch') but Volumnia takes it in its normal sense of 'belonging to the human race'.

18 *foxship* low cunning

24 *in Arabia* (that is, in the desert, where the Tribunes would not have a crowd of plebeians behind them)

31 *unknit* untied

32 *The noble knot* the close bond, of service on his part and gratitude on the part of Rome, which held them together

34 *Cats* (used as a term of contempt – Volumnia's feminine equivalent for the word 'curs' that her son is so fond of using)

48 *told them home* rebuked them thoroughly, given them a piece of your mind

52 *faint puling* feeble whimpering

53 *Juno-like* resembling Juno (the chief goddess of the Romans and wife of Jupiter)

V.3   This little scene, involving two minor characters who do not appear elsewhere in the play, acts as a kind of prologue to the final movement of the action which is now about to begin. Set, as it is, somewhere between Rome and Antium, it indicates the direction in which events are moving and brings the wars between Rome and the Volsces back into the story. More important still, it introduces the idea of treachery which is to have a dominant function in this last phase of the play.

4–5   *my services are, as you are, against 'em* I am in your pay. The treachery of this Roman anticipates the treachery of Coriolanus.

9   *favour* face, countenance
    *approved.* The Folio reads: 'appear'd'. The objections to this reading, which some commentators explain as 'made manifest', are that it is not used elsewhere by Shakespeare as a transitive verb and that it does not give the required sense. Adrian is not too sure of Nicanor's face, but his half-recollection of it is approved (that is, confirmed or reinforced) by his memory of Nicanor's voice.

28   *them* the Volsces

33   *He cannot choose* he is bound to

39   *centurions* officers each of whom commanded a century (see note to I.7.3)

39–40   *their charges* the troops under their command

40   *distinctly billeted* separately enrolled, on a list giving each man's name
    *in th'entertainment* receiving pay

43   *present* immediate

IV.4   This scene and IV.5 are really one continuous scene set at Aufidius's house in Antium. The material on which they are based is derived, with some elaboration, from North, whose account of the hero's entry into Antium

235

and of his meeting with Aufidius is already highly dramatic (*Shakespeare's Plutarch*, pp. 334-8).

(stage direction) *Enter Coriolanus in mean apparel, disguised and muffled.* This graphic stage-direction gives an impression of utter poverty and dereliction, whereas North is very explicit that Coriolanus has only put on this *mean apparel* as a disguise.

3    *'fore my wars* in the face of my attacks

12-26    *O world, thy slippery turns! Friends now fast sworn ... service.* This soliloquy, the most important of the very few that occur in the play, is not a piece of reflection, still less of self-examination. It is rather an attempt by Coriolanus to find some sort of justification for embarking on a course of action that he has decided to undertake without properly understanding his own motives. He adopts a pose of complete cynicism which is foreign both to his nature and to his training.

12    *slippery turns* fickle changes

17    *On a dissension of a doit* over some dispute about the merest trifle

19-20    *Whose passions and whose plots have broke their sleep | To take the one the other* whose passions have kept them awake at night plotting how to destroy each other

22    *interjoin their issues* unite their designs

23-4    *My birthplace hate I, and my love's upon | This enemy town.* The paradoxical quality of this statement emphasizes the 'unnaturalness' of the feeling it expresses.

25    *give me way* grant my request, fall in with my plans


IV.5.2    *fellows* fellow-servants

8-9    *go to the door* get out

14    *companions* rogues, rascals

17    *th' art* thou art (colloquial)

18    *brave* insolent

25    *avoid* leave, quit

32    *station* place to stand in

34      *batten* grow fat

40      *the canopy* the sky (compare *Hamlet*, II.2.303-4, 'this
        most excellent canopy, the air')

44      *kites and crows* (these birds are scavengers, living on
        carrion)

46      *daws* proverbially foolish birds

48-50   *meddle*. There is a quibble here. In the first case 'meddle'
        has the normal meaning of 'interfere', but in the second
        it carries the sense of 'have illicit sexual relations'.

52      *trencher* plate or platter

64      *tackle* rigging of a ship (referring to Coriolanus's dress)

65      *vessel* (used in two senses: (1) ship; (2) the body as the
        vessel that contains the soul)

68-104  *My name ... service*. This speech is very close to
        North's prose (see *Shakespeare's Plutarch*, p. 337),
        which it follows at times almost word for word.

71      *painful* arduous

74      *memory* reminder, memorial

85      *in mere spite* out of pure spite

86      *To be full quit of* to settle my account completely with,
        to get my own back on

88      *of wreak* ready for revenge

        *that wilt* so that you are eager to

89-90   *stop those maims | Of shame* close up those shameful
        wounds

90      *through* throughout

94      *cankered* corrupted

95      *under fiends* devils of hell

96      *prove* try

111     *grainèd ash* tough lance (*grainèd* means straight-grained,
        a straight-grained shaft being stronger than a cross-
        grained one)

112     *clip* embrace

113     *The anvil of my sword*. These words refer to Coriolanus,
        whose armour the sword of Aufidius has so often struck
        like the blows of a hammer on an anvil. Compare the
        First Player's lines in *Hamlet* (II.2.483-6):

> *And never did the Cyclops' hammers fall*
> *On Mars's armour, forged for proof eterne,*
> *With less remorse than Pyrrhus' bleeding sword*
> *Now falls on Priam.*

119      *dances* sets dancing
           *rapt* enraptured

123      *target* shield
           *brawn* muscular arm

124      *out* outright, thoroughly

125      *several* separate, different

134      *o'erbear't.* The Folio reads: 'o're-beate', but an object to the verb is clearly required, and 'o'erbear' is a favourite word of Shakespeare's to describe the action of a flood (compare III.1.248).

139      *absolute* incomparable

141      *commission* command
           *set down* decide, appoint

153–4      *gave me* suggested to me

156–7      *set up a top* start a top spinning

166–7      *a greater soldier than he you wot one* you know of one greater soldier than he

169      *it's no matter for that* never mind about that

192      *directly* without ambiguity

193      *scotched* slashed

194      *carbonado* rasher for grilling

196      *boiled.* Many editors emend to 'broiled', because carbonadoes were broiled. But boiling seems just as likely a method for cannibals to adopt in preparing their victims for the table.

198      *he is so made on* he is made so much of

199      *at upper end* (in the place of honour)

201      *bald* bare-headed. Elizabethan men normally kept their hats on when indoors.

202      *sanctifies himself with's hand* touches his hand as though it were a sacred relic. The language is that of Elizabethan love poetry and may be compared with Romeo's words

to Juliet, 'If I profane with my unworthiest hand | This holy shrine', *Romeo and Juliet*, I.5.93-4.

204    *bottom* essential part, gist

207    *sowl* pull, lug

209    *polled* shorn, stripped bare

215    *directitude*. As the First Servingman's question indicates, this word is a verbal blunder, a piece of nonsense resulting from the speaker's desire to be impressive. He does not know what it means himself, but obviously intends to imply something like 'discredit'.

218    *in blood* in good condition, full of hope and vigour

219    *conies* rabbits

221    *presently* immediately

223    *parcel* part, portion

229-30 *It's sprightly walking, audible, and full of vent.* War is imagined here as a hunting-dog, walking along in a sprightly manner, giving tongue, and eager to pick up the scent of its quarry. Compare 'the dogs of war', *Julius Caesar*, III.1.273.

231    *mulled* stupefied, dull

IV.6    The first part of this scene, up to the entrance of the Aedile at line 37, is of Shakespeare's own invention and forms an ironical contrast with what is to follow. The latter part of it is based loosely on Plutarch.

2    *His remedies are tame* the remedies against Coriolanus are tame. Sicinius is still thinking of Coriolanus as a disease, just as he did in III.1, and is contrasting the wild state of the people then, when they served as an antidote to him, with their present peaceful condition. The Folio reads: 'His remedies are tame, the present peace,' which many editors emend to 'His remedies are tame. The present peace', taking 'His remedies' as 'his means of redress'.

10    *stood to't* made a stand, put up a fight

33    *assistance* associates, partners

34–5   *We should by this, to all our lamentation . . . found it so.*
In this sentence *should* carries the sense of 'should have', owing to the introduction of the conditional clause with *had*.

45   *inshelled* drawn in

47   *what* why

49   *break* break terms

52   *reason with* talk with, question

54   *information* source of information

59   *coming* coming in. Many editors emend to 'come' in order to avoid the jingling effect after *going* at the end of line 58.

61   *raising* incitement, starting of a rumour

63   *seconded* supported

68   *as spacious as between* big enough to include

73   *atone* become reconciled

74   *violent'st contrariety* opposite extremes

79   *O'erborne their way* crushed everything in their way

82   *holp* helped

83   *city leads* lead-covered roofs of the city

86   *in their cement* down to their foundations

88   *auger's bore* the small hole made with an auger

96   *flies.* This reading is taken from the Folio. It results in an awkward repetition, and may well have been produced by the compositor's eye catching the end of the previous line – 'Butter-flies' – in the manuscript he was working from. The present editor thinks, for two reasons, that Shakespeare may well have written 'calves'. First, because calves were closely associated with butchers in his mind – see *Love's Labour's Lost*, V.2. 253–5, *2 Henry VI*, IV.2.26 and, above all, III.1.210–12:

> And as the butcher takes away the calf,
> And binds the wretch, and beats it when it strays,
> Bearing it to the bloody slaughter-house. . . .

Secondly, because the alliterative pattern of lines 94–6, with its heavy use of the letter 'b', seems to demand a word that alliterates with 'confidence' and 'killing' to complete it.

97     *apron-men* 'mechanicals', manual workers who wore leather aprons

98     *the voice of occupation* the votes of handicraftsmen

101     *As Hercules did shake down mellow fruit.* The last of the twelve labours of Hercules was to obtain the golden apples from a tree in the Hesperides (the end of the world) which was guarded by a dragon.

105     *who resists* whoever resist

114     *charged* would be entreating

116     *showed* would appear

119     *made fair hands* made a fine job of it (ironical)

120     *crafted* (used in two senses: (1) carried out a piece of work; (2) intrigued, acted craftily)

124     *clusters* crowds, mob

127     *obeys his points* obeys him in every point

136     *coxcombs* fools' heads

139     *coal* piece of charcoal

150     *cry* pack of hounds

162–3   *Would half my wealth | Would buy this for a lie!* How gladly would I give half my fortune to prove this a lie!


IV.7     A striking feature of Shakespeare's dramatic art is its economy, of which this scene is an excellent example. Based partly on North (*Shakespeare's Plutarch*, pp. 347–8), it serves two different purposes. Its first function is to explain the reasons for Aufidius's turning against Coriolanus, and so to prepare the way for the catastrophe. But Shakespeare also takes this opportunity to sum up his hero's character, as it has appeared so far, and to give a number of possible interpretations of his earlier behaviour, and especially of his failure in the central movement of the action.

5     *darkened* eclipsed, put in the shade

      *action* campaign

6       *by your own* by your own action (in making Coriolanus his fellow-general)

7       *means* remedies (against Coriolanus)

8       *more proudlier.* Shakespeare often uses double comparatives and superlatives in order to give added emphasis. Compare *more worthier* (III.1.120).

11      *changeling* fickle thing

13      *for your particular* where your own interests are concerned

15      *Have* would have. Most editors emend to 'had' in order to bring the construction into line with 'had' in line 13 and again in line 16; but this kind of shift in construction is a fairly common feature of Shakespeare's later style. *borne the action of yourself* conducted the campaign alone, by yourself

22      *husbandry for* management of, concern for the welfare of

23      *achieve* accomplish his intention

34-5    *As is the osprey to the fish, who takes it | By sovereignty of nature.* This is an allusion to the belief that fish, recognizing the kingly status of the osprey, turned up the whites of their bellies to him so that he might seize them more easily.

35-53   *First he was . . . done.* In these lines Aufidius's role is almost that of a Chorus, providing explanations for Coriolanus's actions and at the same time insisting on his 'merit'. The inconclusive nature of the analysis suggests that Shakespeare wishes his audience to realize that there is an element of mystery at the heart of the tragedy.

37      *even* without losing his balance. The idea expressed is almost a repetition of Sicinius's words at II.1.216-17:

> He cannot temperately transport his honours
> From where he should begin and end. . . .

38-9    *out of daily fortune ever taints | The happy man* as a result of uninterrupted success always infects the fortunate man

242

40   *disposing of* making the best use of

43   *casque* helmet (representing the military life)
     *cushion* seat of office (representing the civil life)

44   *austerity and garb* austere manner, rigid discipline

45-7  *but one of these . . . feared.* Having suggested three pos-
      sible reasons for Coriolanus's failure, Aufidius goes on
      to say that one of his explanations, not all of them, must
      be the right one, but he cannot say which it is, because
      to the observer the hero shows traces of them all.

46   *spices* touches, traces

47   *free* absolve

48   *a merit* (that is, his valour)

49   *To choke it in the utterance* to choke any mention of the
      one fatal fault before it can be spoken

49-55  *So our virtues . . . fail.* The best commentary on this
      difficult passage, which is concerned with the transient
      and insecure nature of human achievement, is provided
      by Ulysses's great speech, 'Time hath, my lord, a
      wallet at his back . . .', in *Troilus and Cressida*, III.3.
      145-80.

50   *Lie in th'interpretation of the time* are at the mercy of any
      construction the world chooses to set on them

51-3  *And power, unto itself most commendable . . . done* and
      power, which carries its own commendation with it so
      long as it is active, has no more certain grave than
      the public acknowledgement of its achievements. The
      basic idea is that men's awareness of great deeds can
      only be kept alive by more great deeds; as soon as deeds
      are transformed into words, they lose their lustre and
      become tarnished. Moreover, success leads to defeat.

52   *evident* inevitable, certain; *chair* public rostrum from
      which speeches are made

54-5  *One fire drives out one fire; one nail one nail; | Rights by
      rights fuller, strengths by strengths do fail.* These two lines
      are made up of proverbial statements. The first two are
      to be found in M. P. Tilley's *Dictionary of the Proverbs
      in England in the Sixteenth and Seventeenth Centuries*,

where they appear as F. 277 and N. 17. The fourth is in Erasmus's *Adagia* (949 C), where it is given in the following form: *Fortis in alium fortiorem incidit. Dici solitum, ubi quis nimium fretus suis viribus, aliquando nanciscitur, a quo vincatur.* 'The strong man meets a stronger. Usually said when a man who relies too much on his own unaided power eventually lights on one who proves too much for him.' The present editor has been unable to trace the third, but it must be parallel with the others. The central idea in each case is that any force can only be overcome by a stronger force of the same kind. For this reason the reading *fuller* is adopted in line 55 in place of the Folio's 'fouler', giving the sense 'rights are frustrated by stronger rights, strengths by greater strengths'. For *fuller* meaning 'stronger' compare *Othello*, II.1.6, 'A fuller blast ne'er shook our battlements'. Most editors emend 'fouler' to 'falter'.

V.1  Plutarch relates how the near approach of Coriolanus's forces to Rome 'appeased the sedition and dissension betwixt the nobility and the people' to such an extent that the Senate agreed to the people's demand that his banishment should be repealed. They therefore sent ambassadors to him, choosing for the purpose 'Martius' familiar friends and acquaintance'. Shakespeare heightens the dramatic effect by replacing the nameless friends of his source with Cominius and Menenius, and by sending them separately, instead of as members of the same delegation (see *Shakespeare's Plutarch*, pp. 345–7).

3  *In a most dear particular* with the warmest personal affection

5  *knee* make your way on your knees. Shakespeare has in mind the behaviour of Christian penitents when approaching shrines.

6–7  *coyed* | *To hear* showed disdain when hearing

244

14     *i'th'fire*. The Folio reads 'a'th'fire', but forging is done in a fire, not out of it.

16     *wracked for*. Menenius, who is given to coining words, has here combined 'wrack', meaning 'ruin', with 'rack', meaning 'make a great effort', and produced a portmanteau word, signifying 'toiled to disastrous effect'. Many editors read 'wrecked fair', and others 'racked for'.

17     *memory* memorial

20     *bare* bare-faced, impudent

23     *offered* tried, ventured

28     *nose th'offence* smell the offensive matter

35     *In this so-never-needed help* in this crisis when help was never so badly needed as it is now

38     *instant army* army mobilized on the spur of the moment

45     *grief-shot* stricken with grief

47-8     *after the measure | As you intended well* in proportion to your good intentions

50     *hum at* say 'hum' to (a sign of displeasure)

51     *taken well* approached at the right time. It is characteristic of Menenius, the *bon viveur*, that he should attach so much importance to a good dinner as a means of putting a man in an amiable frame of mind.

55     *conveyances* channels

58     *dieted to* in the mood – following a good meal – to listen to

62     *Speed how it will* let it turn out as it will, no matter what the upshot may be

64     *sit in gold* sit on a golden chair. North writes: '. . . he was set in his chair of state, with a marvellous and an unspeakable majesty' (*Shakespeare's Plutarch*, p. 347).

65     *his injury* his sense of the wrong done to him

70     *Bound with an oath*. This phrase applies equally to both sets of conditions (the concessions he is willing to make and the concessions he is unwilling to make), which, Coriolanus has sworn, must be accepted completely by the Romans.

72  *Unless* except for, if it were not for. Compare *All's Well that Ends Well*, IV.1.4–6: '... we must not seem to understand him, unless some one among us, whom we must produce for an interpreter'.

V.2  This scene, set in the Volscian camp before Rome, has a double function. With its mixture of humour and pathos, it acts as a contrast to the sustained tension of the great scene that is to follow it. At the same time it depicts a further sapping of the hero's resolution. Cominius, his old general, has not left Coriolanus entirely unmoved – ''Twas very faintly he said "Rise". . . .' Now Menenius, who has been the nearest thing to a father that Coriolanus has ever known, touches his feelings even more closely and, in doing so, prepares the ground for the arrival of his family.

(stage direction) *Watch* sentries, military guard

10  *lots to blanks* a thousand to one (referring to lottery tickets)

13  *passable* current, valid (with a pun on 'giving the right to pass')

14  *lover* dearest friend

17  *varnishèd*. The Folio reading 'verified' is unsatisfactory, because it does not connect in any way – as it should – with *size*. *Varnishèd*, probably spelled 'vernished' in the manuscript, does, and gives a typically Shakespearian pun, since *size* means not only magnitude but also the sticky wash used by artists.

19  *lapsing* slipping, collapsing

20  *upon a subtle ground* on a tricky green

21  *tumbled past the throw* overshot the mark

22  *stamped the leasing* given falsehood the stamp of truth

29  *factionary on the party of* active in the support of

40  *front* confront, oppose

43  *dotant* dotard

50  *use me with estimation* treat me with respect

58–9     *say an errand for you* deliver the message for you. Menenius intends to have his say first.

60     *Jack guardant* Jack-in-office on guard
           *office* officiously withhold

61–2     *Guess but my entertainment with him. If.* Many editors emend to 'Guess but by my . . . him if'.

69     *hardly* with difficulty

71     *your gates* the gates of your native city

75     *block* (punning on: (1) obstruction; (2) blockhead)

79     *servanted* put in subjection

79–80     *I owe | My revenge properly* my revenge is my own affair

80     *remission* power to pardon

81–3     *That we have been familiar . . . much* the ungrateful forgetfulness of my services, which you and the Roman nobility have shown, shall poison the memory of our friendship rather than that I will allow any sense of pity to remind me of how great that friendship was

94     *shent* rebuked

100     *slight* insignificant, worthless
           *by himself* by his own hand

102     *long* for a long time

105–6     *The worthy fellow is our general. He's the rock, the oak not to be wind-shaken* (a most powerful piece of unconscious irony)

V.3     Deeply indebted to North, whom Shakespeare follows almost word for word when writing Volumnia's appeal to her son, this scene is the climax of the play. The setting for it is described in some detail by the source, which runs as follows (*Shakespeare's Plutarch*, pp. 352–3):

> *Now was Martius set then in his chair of state, with all the honours of a general; and, when he had spied the women coming afar off, he marvelled what the matter*

*meant; but afterwards, knowing his wife, which came foremost, he determined at the first to persist in his obstinate and inflexible rancour. But overcome in the end with natural affection, and being altogether altered to see them, his heart would not serve him to tarry their coming to his chair, but, coming down in haste, he went to meet them; and first he kissed his mother and embraced her a pretty while, then his wife and little children; and nature so wrought with him that the tears fell from his eyes, and he could not keep himself from making much of them, but yielded to the affection of his blood, as if he had been violently carried with the fury of a most swift-running stream.*

3    *plainly* openly, straightforwardly

11    *godded* idolized, made a god of
      *latest refuge* last resource

15–17    *And cannot now accept, to grace him only | That thought he could do more. A very little | I have yielded to.* Many editors read: 'And cannot now accept. To . . . more, a . . . to.'

16–17    *A very little | I have yielded to* I did not yield much

20–37    *Shall I be tempted to infringe my vow . . . kin.* These lines must be an aside, since the hero is not likely to reveal intimate feelings of this kind either to the Volsces or to the suppliants.

21    (stage direction) *Enter Virgilia, Volumnia, Valeria, young Martius, with Attendants.* Many editors add the words 'in mourning habits' after 'Enter', though there is no clear indication either in the text or in North that the women are so dressed. From what Volumnia says at lines 94–6, rags would seem to be more appropriate.

25    *bond and privilege of nature* the natural ties of love and affection that bind the family together

26    *obstinate* hard-hearted

30    *Olympus* (mountain in Greece, home of the gods in classical mythology)

32    *aspect of intercession* pleading look

38    *These eyes are not the same I wore in Rome* I see things differently now

39    *delivers* presents

41    *out* at fault. For this use of the word *out* in a technical theatrical sense, see *Love's Labour's Lost*, V.2.149–72.

46    *the jealous queen* (Juno, the guardian of marriage)

48    *virgined it* remained chaste
      *pray.* Many editors emend to 'prate', but Coriolanus has just sworn by Juno and may, therefore, well think of himself as praying. Moreover, 'prate' is an ugly word with which to describe the tender adoration with which he has just greeted Virgilia.

51    *more impression* a deeper mark (both metaphorically and literally)

52–6  *O, stand up blest! | ... parent.* This speech is deliberately ironical. Volumnia knows precisely how to exert pressure on her son.

52    *blest* lucky, fortunate

54    *unproperly* unfittingly, against all propriety

57    *corrected son* the son whom you have chastised

58    *hungry* barren. The essential idea behind the passage is that a reversal of the whole natural order of things is taking place when a pebble, one of the most insignificant things in creation, can strike, or show contempt for, the stars.

61    *Murdering impossibility* making nothing seem impossible

64    *Publicola* (traditionally one of the first consuls of Rome, in 509 B.C. He is the subject of one of Plutarch's *Lives*.)

66    *curdied* congealed

67    *Dian* (Diana, goddess of chastity)

68    *epitome* abridgement of a book or discourse

69    *by th'interpretation of full time.* Time is imaged as a preacher or scholar developing a complete discourse from his 'epitome' or notes.

70    *The god of soldiers* (Mars)

73    *To shame unvulnerable* incapable of dishonour
      *stick* stand firm and stand out

74      *sea-mark* conspicuous object serving as a navigational
        guide to sailors
        *standing* withstanding
        *flaw* gust of wind, sudden storm

80      *forsworn to grant* sworn not to grant

81      *Be held by you denials* be regarded by you as a refusal
        to answer your requests

82      *capitulate* parley, discuss terms

83      *mechanics* workmen, handicraftsmen (used here in a
        contemptuous sense to mean 'low fellows, rabble')

90      *fail in* fail to grant

95      *bewray* reveal

103     *to poor we*. Shakespeare occasionally uses *we* where
        modern usage would require 'us'. Compare the words
        of Brutus after the killing of Caesar: 'and let no man
        abide this deed | But we the doers' (*Julius Caesar*, III.1.
        94–5).

104     *capital* fatal, deadly

112     *evident* certain, inevitable

114     *foreign recreant* traitorous deserter to a foreign state

119     *purpose* propose, intend

120     *determine* end

121     *grace* favour, mercy

124     *Trust to't, thou shalt not* be sure you shall not march
        without treading

127     *'A* he (colloquial)

129–30  *Not of a woman's tenderness to be | Requires nor child nor
        woman's face to see.* Coriolanus means: 'I shall grow
        effeminate and womanish if I do not stop looking at
        them.' The rhyme has the effect of giving the statement
        a gnomic quality.

129–31  *Not of . . . long* (probably spoken as an aside)

136     *while* so that at the same time

139     *the all-hail* a general acclamation

146     *it* his reputation for nobility

149–53  *Thou hast affected the fine strains of honour . . . oak.*
        These lines are a statement of what Volumnia wishes

her son to say: namely, that he has given the impression of pursuing revenge out of over-refined sentiments of personal honour, in order that in the end he may behave like Jove, who terrifies men with his thunder, but, in his mercy, only directs his lightning at an oak.

151   *the wide cheeks o'th'air.* Maps in Shakespeare's time depicted the four winds issuing from the swollen cheeks of cherubs.

152   *sulphur* lightning
      *bolt* thunderbolt

153   *rive* split

157   *childishness* (the natural instinctive appeal to the affections that a child has)

162   *fond of* wishing for

166   *honest* honest with yourself, truthful

167   *restrain'st* keep back, withhold

170   *'longs* belongs, is due

176   *reason* argue for

179   *his child.* Some editors emend to 'this child'.

182   (stage direction) *Holds her by the hand, silent.* Shakespeare found the hint for this direction – one of the most telling in any of his plays – in North, whose narrative he alters subtly at this point in a way that makes it far more dramatic. The source runs (*Shakespeare's Plutarch*, p. 357):

> *And with these words herself, his wife, and children fell down upon their knees before him. Martius, seeing that, could refrain no longer, but went straight and lift her up, crying out:*
>   *'Oh mother, what have you done to me?'*
> *And holding her hard by the right hand,*
>   *'Oh mother,' said he, 'you have won a happy victory for your country, but mortal and unhappy for your son. For I see myself vanquished by you alone.'*

190   *mortal* fatally

191   *true* according to my promise

192    *convenient* proper, appropriate
195    *withal* by it
203    *former fortune* fortune like my former one
205    *which* (that is, the treaty)
208    *a temple built you.* Here Shakespeare has worked in a later passage from North, describing how the grateful Senate decided to grant the ladies whatever they should ask for: 'And they only requested that they would build a Temple of Fortune of the Women' (*Shakespeare's Plutarch*, p. 359).


V.4    As a prelude to the catastrophe, Shakespeare moves the action back to Rome once more for some final ironies. Menenius's picture of Coriolanus is a sketch of him as he was, not as he is. But the behaviour of the people has not altered – they are as variable as they ever were.

7–8    *stay upon* wait for
11     *differency* dissimilarity
19     *engine* instrument of war – probably a battering-ram
21     *his hum* his way of saying 'hum'
       *battery* military assault
       *state* throne, chair of state
21–2   *as a thing made for Alexander* like a statue of Alexander the Great
26     *in the character* to the life
29     *'long of you* because of you
36     *hale* drag, pull
40     *are dislodged* have left their positions (military term)
46     *blown tide* tide driven by the wind. Shakespeare may well have been thinking of the tide, with an east wind behind it, racing through the arches of London Bridge.
48–9   *The trumpets, sackbuts, psalteries, and fifes,* | *Tabors and cymbals.* This list of musical instruments was probably suggested by the biblical catalogue (Daniel, 3.5): 'the cornet, flute, harp, sackbut, psaltery, dulcimer, and all kinds of music'.

48    *sackbuts* bass trumpets rather like trombones
      *psalteries* stringed instruments

56    (stage direction) *Sound still with the shouts* (a command
      to those responsible for noises off in Shakespeare's
      theatre)

V.5   There is, of course, no change of location and no proper
      scene division. All that happens is that Sicinius and the
      Messenger go off on one side of the stage to meet the
      procession, and return with it. The scene is the ironical
      counterpart to Coriolanus's return in II.1. Then Rome
      rejoiced over his victory; now it rejoices over his defeat
      – by his mother.

5     *Repeal him* recall him from exile

V.6   In Plutarch Coriolanus returns to Antium after yielding
      to his mother, and it is there that he meets his death
      (*Shakespeare's Plutarch*, pp. 360–62). It seems as though
      Shakespeare began this final scene with the same loca-
      tion in mind, for at line 50 the First Conspirator
      describes the place as Aufidius's *native town*, and there
      are further references to Antium – none of them very
      obvious – at line 73 and line 80. Then, when Shake-
      speare came to write Aufidius's speech beginning at
      line 88, he suddenly realized in the course of composi-
      tion how much more dramatically appropriate Corioles
      would be, and made the switch, knowing that no
      audience would have noticed the earlier references to
      Antium. The play has come full circle. Once again
      Coriolanus is back at the scene of his victory, 'alone', as
      he was in I.4, 'To answer all the city'.

4     *theirs* their. This use of *theirs* as a pronominal adjective
      before the noun has been explained as follows: 'It is
      felt that the ear cannot wait till the end of the sentence
      while so slight a word as *her* or *their* remains with

nothing to depend on' (E. A. Abbott, *A Shakespearian Grammar*, London, 1884, p. 161).

5      *Him* he whom

6      *ports* gates

14     *parties* supporters

15     *Of* out of

17–19   *The people will remain uncertain whilst . . . all.* The Volscian mob, Shakespeare emphasizes, is as unstable as the Roman mob.

18     *difference* disagreement

20–21   *admits* | *A good construction* is capable of a good interpretation

22     *truth* loyalty

       *heightened* exalted

23     *plants* (used figuratively for position and dignities)

26     *free* outspoken

27     *stoutness* obstinate pride

32     *gave him way* gave way to him

34     *files* ranks

35     *designments* undertakings, enterprises

37     *end* gather in as a harvest

40–41   *He waged me with his countenance as if* | *I had been mercenary* he paid me with his patronage as though I were a hired soldier. It is Coriolanus's natural and habitual assumption of authority that galls Aufidius

43     *had carried* might have taken

44     *There was it* that was the thing

45     *my sinews shall be stretched upon him* my forces shall be strained to the utmost against him

50     *post* messenger

54     *at your vantage* seizing your opportunity

57     *along* stretched out dead

58     *After your way his tale pronounced* the story of his actions as you will tell it

59     *reasons* version of the matter

64     *made* committed

65     *easy fines* light punishment

67    *levies* work of raising an army
       *answering* repaying

68    *charge* expenses

73    *hence* (from Antium, which he left at the end of IV.5)
       *subsisting* continuing

75    *prosperously I have attempted* my efforts have proved successful

78    *Doth more than counterpoise a full third part* exceed by more than a third

84    *compounded* reached an agreement

85    *traitor in the highest degree* traitor of the most criminal kind. Compare *Richard III*, V.3.196: 'Perjury, perjury, in the highest degree.'

93    *drops of salt* the tears of Volumnia and Virgilia, which Aufidius has already described (line 46) as *drops of women's rheum*

95    *oath and resolution* sworn purpose

96    *twist* plaited thread

96–7  *never admitting | Counsel o'th'war* never taking counsel of his fellow-officers

99    *heart* courage

100   *others* the others

102   *No more* (that is, no more than a boy)

107   *his own notion* his own sense of the truth

113   *edges* swords

114   *there* recorded there

118   *blind fortune* sheer good luck

121   *presently* at once

127   *judicious* judicial, according to law
       *Stand* stop

128–30 *O that I had him . . . sword!* His mother's son to the last, Coriolanus almost repeats her words to Sicinius at IV.2.23–5.

131   (stage direction) *The Conspirators draw their swords, and kill. . . .* The Folio reads: '*Draw both the Conspirators, and kils*'.

139   *did owe you* had for you

141   *deliver* show

146   *impatience* rage, anger

150   *I'll be one.* I'll be the fourth – four being the usual num-
      ber required to remove a corpse decently from the stage.
      Compare *Hamlet*, V.2.387–8: 'Let four captains | Bear
      Hamlet like a soldier'.

152   *Trail your steel pikes.* At military funerals in Elizabethan
      England the trained bands of the City carried their
      pikes at the trail (that is, with the butt-end near the
      ground and the point sloping forward) as a sign of
      mourning.

153   *unchilded* deprived of children

155   *a noble memory.* North writes (*Shakespeare's Plutarch*,
      p. 362):

> *Howbeit it is a clear case, that this murder was not
> generally consented unto of the most part of the Volsces.
> For men came out of all parts to honour his body, and
> did honourably bury him, setting out his tomb with great
> store of armour and spoils, as the tomb of a worthy
> person and great captain.*

It is with just this impression of his hero's nobility and
greatness that Shakespeare seeks to leave his audience.

# AN ACCOUNT OF THE TEXT

STILL unpublished when Shakespeare died in 1616, *Coriolanus* is one of the seventeen plays that were printed for the first time in the First Folio of 1623, where it was originally intended to stand at the head of the Tragedies, a position which it later lost through the last-minute inclusion of *Troilus and Cressida* in the volume. Since its publication was quite regular, this version, with the authority of Shakespeare's old friends and fellow-actors, John Heminge and Henry Condell, to back it, is the sole source for the text of the play.

There are strong indications that the material Heminge and Condell placed at the printers' disposal was either a carefully prepared manuscript in Shakespeare's autograph – probably a fair copy – or a close transcript of it. In the first place, *Coriolanus* is unusually long for an Elizabethan play, and it seems unlikely that it would normally have been produced in its entirety. The prompt-copy would, therefore, have been a cut version, which the Folio text plainly is not. Secondly, the stage directions, while exceptionally detailed and elaborate, are in many cases of a kind that would not have been convenient in an actual performance, and appear to have been written for the benefit of a producer rather than as commands to the actors. The opening of the third scene provides a good example: '*Enter Volumnia and Virgilia, mother and wife to Martius: they set them down on two low stools and sew.*' This is the kind of business that is generally left to actors in rehearsal, and its inclusion suggests that when Shakespeare wrote the play he was no longer in such close touch with the company as he had been hitherto – perhaps he was already spending most of his time at Stratford. Furthermore, many of the directions are too indefinite to serve for a performance. '*Enter seven or eight Citizens*', at the beginning of II.3, and '*Enter three or four Conspirators of Aufidius's faction*', at

V.6.8, leave things vague which the actors need to know. Some of the directions, such as that which introduces I.7, even have a distinct literary quality about them and look like the author's sketch for the action and dialogue that are to follow. Finally, there are a number of spellings which seem to be peculiar to Shakespeare. The form 'Scicinius' for 'Sicinius', which occurs in the stage direction at II.3.137 and consistently as a speech heading for the rest of the scene, as well as spasmodically in III.1, looks like a close relation of the unusual spelling 'scilens' for 'silence', which is to be found at line 50 of Shakespeare's part of the play *Sir Thomas More* (the only piece of dramatic writing in his own hand that still survives) and which appears no fewer than eighteen times in the Quarto version of *2 Henry IV*, published in 1600, where it stands for the name of the character Silence.

But, while there is good evidence that the Folio text of *Coriolanus* was set from Shakespeare's autograph, there must have been some editorial interference with the manuscript before it reached the printer. The mark of it is to be seen in some of the punctuation. For instance, the Folio text at III.3.68–74 runs as follows (here the 'long s' [ʃ] is replaced by 's' in all quotations):

> The fires i'th'lowest hell. Fould in the people:
> Call me their Traitor, thou iniurious Tribune.
> Within thine eyes sate twenty thousand deaths
> In thy hands clutcht: as many Millions in
> Thy lying tongue, both numbers. I would say
> Thou lyest vnto thee, with a voice as free,
> As I do pray the Gods.

This pointing is clearly the work of someone who simply did not understand the sense of the passage he was dealing with, and cannot therefore be Shakespeare's. The punctuation is, in fact, one of the most difficult of the problems that face the editor of this play.

There are two others. First, there is a good deal of mislineation, or what appears to be mislineation, of the verse. Quite often one speech ends with a half-line and the next begins with a full line, and it is not easy to be sure whether the resulting irregularity is deliberate or not. For example, I.9.19–23 in the present edition appears in the following form in the Folio:

> Hath ouerta'ne mine Act.
>    *Com.* You shall not be the Graue of your deseruing,
> Rome must know the value of her owne:
> 'Twere a Concealement worse then a Theft,
> No less then a Traducement,
> To hide your doings, and to silence that. . . .

By using the words 'You shall not be' to complete the previous half-line, the metre can be smoothed out, but this procedure does involve the loss of the emphasis which Cominius's three lines 'Rome . . . Traducement' acquire from the heavy stresses and pauses which are needed to eke them out. Shakespeare's blank verse in his last period is such a flexible medium that only the insensitive can be dogmatic about it.

The other main difficulty that the Folio text raises is occasioned by the large number of misprints in it. Most of them can, however, be explained as a natural result of peculiarities in Shakespeare's handwriting, and add weight to the view that the text was set up from his autograph. To take one instance out of many: the appearance of the curious word 'Contenning' at I.3.44, where it looks like the name of the Gentlewoman attending on Valeria, is probably due to his fondness for using a capital 'C' initially and to his carelessness in differentiating between 'm' and 'n'. The word he wrote was almost certainly 'contemning'.

Below are listed departures in the present text of *Coriolanus* from that of the First Folio. Obvious minor misprints are not noted, nor are changes in lineation and punctuation unless they are of special significance. A few of these alterations were made in one of the three seventeenth-century reprints of the Folio (F2, F3, and F4); these are indicated. Most of them were first made by editors during the eighteenth century. Emendations suggested by modern editors are gratefully acknowledged.

In the following instances the emendation is due to the present editor: I.6.42, II.1.236, III.1.187, III.2.21, and IV.7.55.

## COLLATIONS

### I

| | | |
|---|---|---|
| I.1. | 26 | FIRST CITIZEN] *All.* |
| | 33 | SECOND CITIZEN] *All.* |
| | 55 | (and for the rest of the scene) FIRST CITIZEN] *2 Cit.* |
| | 90 | stale't] scale't |
| | 108 | tauntingly] (F2; spelt 'tantingly'); taintingly |
| | 170 | geese. You are no] Geese you are: No |
| | 212 | Shouting] Shooting |
| | 214–15 | Brutus, one \| Sicinius Velutus, and – I] *Brutus,* \| *Sicinius Velutus, and I* |
| | 230 | together.] together? |
| I.3. | 44 | sword, contemning. Tell] sword. *Contenning,* tell |
| I.4. | 42 | trenches. Follow's!] Trenches followes. |
| | 56 | lost] left |
| | 59 | Cato's] *Calues* |
| I.5. | 3 | (stage direction) *Trumpeter*] *Trumpet.* |
| I.6. | 42 | truth – but for our gentlemen.] truth: but for our Gentlemen, |
| | 53 | Antiates] Antients |
| | 76 | O'me alone, make you a sword of me.] Oh me alone, make you a sword of me: |
| | 84 | I] foure |
| I.9. | 49 | shout] (F4); shoot |
| | 64, 66 | Caius Martius] *Marcus Caius* |
| II.1. | 53–4 | I cannot say] I can say |
| | 60 | bisson] beesome |
| | 117–18 | Brings 'a victory in his pocket, the] brings a Victorie in his Pocket? the |
| | 119 | brows, Menenius. He] Browes: *Menenius,* hee |
| | 157–8 | Caius Martius; there \| In honour follows Coriolanus] *Martius Caius:* \| These in honor followes *Martius Caius Coriolanus* |

II.1. 173   CORIOLANUS] *Com.*

196   (stage direction) *Brutus and Sicinius come forward*]
    *Enter Brutus and Scicinius*

226   napless] Naples

236   authority's for an end.] Authorities, for an end.

243   the war] their Warre

II.2. 34   (stage direction) *by themselves*] *by themselues:*
    *Coriolanus stands.*

44   Caius Martius] *Martius Caius*

89   chin] (F3); Shinne

II.3. 36   it. I say, if] it, I say. If

65   Ay, but not mine] I, but mine

113   hire] (F2); higher

114   wolvish toge] Wooluish tongue

242–3   And Censorinus, nobly naméd so, | Twice being by
    the people chosen censor] And Nobly nam'd, so
    twice being Censor

III.1. 91   O good but] O God! but

92   reckless] wreaklesse

143   Where one] Whereon

185–6   Tribunes! . . . Citizens!] Assigned to 2. *Sen.*

187   MENENIUS] *All.*

229   your house] our house

230   CORIOLANUS] *Com.*

236   COMINIUS] (F2); *Corio.*

237–41   CORIOLANUS I would . . . Capitol. MENENIUS
    Be gone . . . another.] *Mene.* I would . . . another.

286   our] one

304   SICINIUS] *Menen.*

322–3   bring him | Where] bring him in peace, | Where

III.2. 21   crossings] things

40–41   noble. | But when extremities speak, I have heard
    you say,] Noble, | But when extremities speake. I
    haue heard you say,

78   With] Which

80   handling, say] handling: or say

115   lulls] lull

III.3.  36   Throng] Through
        55   accents] Actions
       110   for] from
IV.1.   37   VIRGILIA] *Corio.*
IV.2.   17   this, fool:] this Foole,
IV.3.    9   approved] appear'd
IV.4.   23   hate] haue
IV.5.  134   o'erbear't] o're-beate
      192–3   him, directly to say the truth on't. Before Corioles
             he] him directly, to say the Troth on't before
             *Corioles*, he
IV.7.   49   virtues] Vertue
        55   fuller] fouler
V.1.    14   i'th'] a'th'
V.2.    17   varnishèd] (*J. Dover Wilson*); verified
      61–4   Guess but my ... him. If ... suffering, behold]
             guesse but my ... him: if ... suffering, behold
V.3.     0   (stage direction) *Aufidius with others. They sit*]
             *Auffidius.*
     15–17   accept, to grace him only | That thought he could
             do more. A very little | I have yielded to.] accept,
             to grace him onely, | That thought he could do
             more: A very little | I haue yeelded too.
        42   (stage direction) (*Rising and going to her*)] Not in F.
        50   (stage direction) *He kneels*] *Kneeles*
        52   (stage direction) *He rises*] Not in F.
        56   (stage direction) *She kneels*] Not in F.
        57   (stage direction) *He raises her*] Not in F.
        63   holp] hope
        93   (stage direction) (*He sits*)] Not in F.
       131   (stage direction) *He rises*] Not in F.
       152   charge] change
V.6.57–8   second. When he lies along, | After your way his]
             second, when he lies along | After your way. His
       116   Fluttered] (F3); Flatter'd
       131   (stage direction) *The Conspirators draw their swords,
             and kill*] *Draw both the Conspirators, and kils*

262

Below are listed instances where the present edition substantially preserves readings of the First Folio that have often, with some measure of plausibility, been emended, or introduces an emendation that is different from the one normally accepted. Emendations frequently found in modern editions of the play are given after the square bracket.

I.1. 256 him; he] (F1: him, he); him! He

I.4. 42 trenches. Follow's] (F1: Trenches followes); trenches followed

I.5. 4 hours] honours

I.6. 42 truth – but for our gentlemen.] (F1: truth: but for our Gentlemen,); truth. But for our gentlemen,

76 O'me alone, make you a sword of me.] (F1: Oh me alone, make you a sword of me:); O me, alone! Make you a sword of me?

I.9. 40 beheld] upheld (*J. Dover Wilson*)

46 An overture] A coverture

II.1. 178 begin at] begnaw the (*J. Dover Wilson*)

236 authority's for an end.] (F1: Authorities, for an end.); authorities. For an end,

247 teach] touch

II.2. 106 Where it did mark, it took from face to foot.] (F1: Where it did marke, it tooke from face to foot:); Where it did mark, it took; from face to foot

III.1. 48 COMINIUS] CORIOLANUS

III.2. 21 crossings] (F1: things); thwartings; taxings (*C. J. Sisson*)

32 heart] herd

IV.5. 196 boiled] broiled

229 sprightly walking,] sprightly, waking,

IV.6. 2–4 tame – the . . . hurry. Here do we make] tame. The . . . hurry, here do make

59 coming] come

IV.7. 55 fuller] (F1: fouler); falter

V.1.   14   i'th'] (F1: a'th'); o'th' (F4)

        16   wracked for] racked for; wrecked fair

V.2. 61–4  Guess but my . . . him. If . . . suffering, behold]
             (F1: guesse but my . . . him: if . . . suffering, be-
             hold); Guess but by my . . . him if . . . suffering;
             behold

V.3. 15–17 accept, to grace him only | That thought he could
             do more. A very little | I have yielded to.] (F1:
             accept, to grace him onely, | That thought he
             could do more: A very little | I haue yeelded too.);
             accept; to grace him only | That thought he could
             do more, a very little | I have yielded to

        48   pray] prate

     179   his child] this child